Franke Lange

Literacy in Context

Language of
media and the moving image

D1721995

John O'Connor

Media consultant   Graham Charlton

General editors   Joan Ward *and* John O'Connor
Literacy consultant   Lyn Ranson
General consultant   Frances Findlay

PUBLISHED BY THE PRESS SYNDICATE OF THE UNIVERSITY OF CAMBRIDGE
The Pitt Building, Trumpington Street, Cambridge, United Kingdom

CAMBRIDGE UNIVERSITY PRESS
The Edinburgh Building, Cambridge CB2 2RU, UK
40 West 20th Street, New York, NY 10011-4211, USA
10 Stamford Road, Oakleigh, VIC 3166, Australia
Ruiz de Alarcón 13, 28014 Madrid, Spain
Dock House, The Waterfront, Cape Town 8001, South Africa

http://www.cambridge.org

© Cambridge University Press 2001

This book is in copyright. Subject to statutory exception and to the provisions of relevant collective licensing agreements, no reproduction of any part may take place without the written permission of Cambridge University Press.

First published 2001
Second printing 2001

Printed in the United Kingdom at the University Press, Cambridge

Typeface Delima MT 10.5pt on 12.5pt leading   *System* QuarkXPress®

A catalogue record for this book is available from the British Library

ISBN 0 521 80568 6 paperback

Prepared for publication by Pentacor PLC

Cover photograph of John Fleck

Illustrations by Geoff Jones (pp.38, 39, 49, 50, 51, 55, 56, 57, 75), Brian Lee (pp.64, 71) David Shenton (pp.68, 77)

ACKNOWLEDGEMENTS
The publishers gratefully acknowledge the following for permission to reproduce copyright material.

Textual material Newspaper extracts from 'Blair faces villa sleaze probe' (p.8) by Patrick O'Flynn (*Daily Express* 7 Jan. 2000, p.2); 'Hospital faces beds crisis as flu cases soar' (p.8) by Rachel Ellis (*Daily Express* 7 Jan. 2000, p.7); 'New boy Gary scores winner and outshoots Des Lynam' (p.8) by Ben Summerskill (*Daily Express* 7 Jan. 2000, p.23); 'Crimebuster aged just 13, Schoolgirl wages war on crooks' (p.9) by Martin Stote (*Daily Express* 7 Jan. 2000, p.27); 'Hole lotta trouble' (p.11) (*Daily Star* 7 Jan. 2000, p.23); 'Postie's down under blunder' (p.9) (*Daily Star* 7 Jan. 2000 p.23); 'Golfer is beaten black and roo,' selected phrases from the article (p.25) (*Daily Star* 24 Mar. 2000), reproduced by permission of the *Daily Express*. 'Dome sweet Dome...for the people' (p.8) (*Daily Mirror* 7 Jan. 2000, p.7); 'Kate's Mossery man' (p.8) (*Daily Mirror* 7 Jan. 2000, p.19); 'Top of the pups' (p.8) (*Daily Mirror* 7 Jan. 2000, p.11); 'This is the dramatic proof...' (p.23) by Dawn Alford (*Daily Mirror* 29 Feb. 2000), reproduced by permission of the *Daily Mirror*. 'Boy lama flees across Himalayas to escape Chinese' (p.8) (*Daily Telegraph* 7 Jan. 2000, p.1) © Telegraph Group Ltd, 7 January 2000, reproduced by permission of the *Daily Telegraph*. 'Threat of Ice Titan' (p.14, 15) by James Chapman (*Daily Mail* 24 Mar. 2000, p.37), reproduced by permission of Atlantic Syndication on behalf of the *Daily Mail*. 'Beckham sees red once more' (p.9) (*Independent* 7 Jan. 2000, p.1); 'Now at last we have got over our irrational fear of rabies...' (p.23) by John O'Farrell (*Independent* 29 Feb. 2000), reproduced by permission of the *Independent*. 'Stop him' (p.20, 21) by John Kay (*Sun* 24 Mar. 2000, pp.4,5). © News International Newspapers Ltd, 24 Mar. 2000, by permission of the *Sun*. Extracts from *The Hound of the Baskervilles* (pp.63, 70) by Sir Arthur Conan Doyle (Oxford University Press) copyright © 1996 The Sir Arthur Conan Doyle Copyright Holders, by permission of Jonathan Clowes Ltd, London, on behalf of Andrea Plunket, administrator of the Sir Arthur Conan Doyle copyrights; *The Hound of the Baskervilles* (pp.64, 65) by John O'Connor (Nelson Thornes), by permission of Nelson Thornes

Artworks for Holidays in Egypt advertisement (p.26), by permission of The Egyptian Tourist Authority; 'I'll be your Valentine' advertisement (p.26), by permission of the National Canine Defence League; Yorkie advertisement (p.27), by permission of Société des Produits Nestlé S.A.; K Softees advertisement (p.27), by permission of 'Clarkes International'; HP Baked Beans advertisement (p.27), by permission of Willox Ambler Rodford Law; Marwell Zoo brochure (p.27), by permission of Marwell Zoological Park; Fanta advertisement and logo (p.32), by permission of The Coca-Cola Company, 'Fanta' is a registered trademark of The Coca-Cola Company, 'diet Fanta' is a trademark of The Coca-Cola Company; Jacobs Twiglets advertisement (p.33), by permission of Jacobs; Jammy Dodgers television advertisement (p.38, 39) by permission of Burton's Biscuits; Clarks shoes television advertisement, by permission of 'Clarks International'

Photographs MI5 Chief Stephen Lander (p.20), by permission of The Press Association; Laptop, Paddington Station and MI5 headquarters (p.20, 21) Harry Page, by permission of the *Sun*; Somme (p.48) by permission of The Art Archive; Eric Cantona sequence 'As bad as it gets' by permission of *Match of the Day* magazine, BBC; Faces on Marwell Zoo brochure (p.26), by permission of Pebble Graphics Design Consultants; photographer with camera (p.26) by permission of Allsports UK Ltd.

Every effort has been made to trace copyright holders, but in some cases this has proved impossible. The publishers would be happy to hear from any copyright holder that has not been acknowledged.

Introduction

- Read a piece of text
- Read it again to discover what makes it a special kind of writing
- Check that you understand it
- Focus on key features
- Learn about these language features and practise using them
- Improve your spelling
- Plan and write your own similar piece
- Check it and redraft

Each unit in this book helps you to understand more about a particular kind of writing, learn about its language features and work towards your own piece of writing in a similar style.

Grammar, spelling and punctuation activities, based on the extract, will improve your language skills and take your writing to a higher level.

 The book at a glance

The texts

Each part of the book contains units of extracts and activities at different levels to help you measure your progress.

Each unit includes these sections:

Purpose

This explains exactly what you will read, learn about and write.

Key features

These are the main points to note about the way the extract is written.

Language skills

These activities will improve your grammar, punctuation and spelling. They are all based on the extracts. They are organised using the Word, Sentence and Text Level Objectives of the *National Literacy Strategy Framework for Teaching English*.

Planning your own writing

This structured, step-by-step guide will help you to get started, use writing frames and then redraft and improve your work.

Teacher's Portfolio

This includes worksheets for more language practice, revision and homework. Self-assessment charts will help you to judge and record what level you have reached and to set your own targets for improvement!

Contents

Newspapers

Unit	Texts	Text types	Key features
1 **What's in a newspaper?** Pages 8–13	All in a day's work	Newspaper cuttings & a complete article	• Wordplay • Syntax • Different kinds of newspaper article
2 **Reporting the news** Pages 14–19	Iceberg!	Newspaper report	• Variety of expression • Quotes and reported speech • Text structure
3 **Writing for an audience** Pages 20–25	Stop thief!	Newspaper report	• Colloquial language • Sentence structure • Paragraphs

Advertising

Unit	Texts	Text types	Key features
4 **Who needs to advertise?** Pages 26–31	Argos, beans and cornflakes: an ABC of advertising	A selection of advertisements	• The advertisers • Text and image • Advertising media
5 **Selling the product** Pages 32–37	Fanta House and Twiglets Treble	Two magazine advertisements	• Wordplay • Language suited to audience • Words and images
6 **TV advertising and comedy** Pages 38–43	How jammy can you get?	Television advertising	• Structure • Visuals and sound • Humour

Word	Spelling	Sentence	Text	Activities
• Puns • Rhyme	• Silent *w* • *wr-* words	• Sentence subject • Adjectival phrases	• Types of article	Create headlines and opening sentences
• Synonyms	• *gh* and *ght* words	• Quotes	• Content and structure • The intro	Write a newspaper report
• Colloquial language	• ICT words	• Register	• Paragraphs	Write an article in informal register

• Emotive words	• Plurals	• Slogans	• The print media • Advertising sites • Image and copy	Create a magazine advertisement for a charity or a campaign
• Jargon	• Homophones	• Imperative sentences	• Typography • Logos • Graphics	Draft a proposal for a magazine advertisement

Media skills	Activities
• The moving-image media • Humour in television advertising • Genres • Parody • The spelling of loan words	Write an analysis of a television advertisement

Contents

The moving image

Unit	Text	Text types	Key features
7 **Match of the day** Pages 44–49	Kung-fu Cantona	A sequence from a televised football match	• Capturing key moments • Viewing the main incident • Use of cameras
8 **Screen horror** Pages 50–55	*Frankenstein*	Storyboard of the final sequence of a horror film	• Variety of shots • Framing • Cutting
9 **Shakespeare in action** Pages 56–61	Macbeth and the witches	Storyboard of the opening sequence of a film version of Shakespeare	• Adapting the script • Visuals and sound effects

Comparing texts

Unit	Text	Text types	Key features
10 **Book, theatre, radio and cinema** Pages 62–73	*The Hound of the Baskervilles* Arthur Conan Doyle	A novel text A stage dramatisation A radio adaptation A film version	• Stage dramatisation: the use of physical space • Radio adaptation: the use of sound effects and dialogue • Film version: creating images
11 **Ways of selling** Pages 74–79	How to get your new shoes noticed	A magazine advertisement and a television advertisement for the same product	• Message • Image and text in magazine ads • Sequence of scenes in television ads
Glossary Page 80			

Media skills

- Terminology:
  Frame
  Sequence
  Shot
- Editing

- Shots
- Framing
- Cutting
- Montage
- Genres

- Shots
- Framing
- Camera angle
- Interpretation
- Location, props and costumes
- Casting

Activities

Plan to televise an incident from history

Plan a film sequence in a well-known genre

Write an analysis of the opening of a film version of *Macbeth*

- Stage dramatisation:
  Location and
  physical space
  Stage directions
- Radio adaptation:
  Sound effects
  Dialogue
- Film version:
  Montage
  Framing
  Shots

- Target groups
- Message
- Images
- Captions
- Duration

Adapt an extract from *The Hound of the Baskervilles* for radio

Write an article comparing the magazine advertisement with the television advertisement

What's in a newspaper?

1 ▷ **Purpose**

In this unit you will:
- read extracts from newspaper articles
- talk about the different kinds of articles to be found in newspapers
- write your own newspaper headlines and article openings

▷▷ **Subject links:** *PSHE, history, media studies*

2 ▷ **Headlines and articles**

All in a day's work

All of these articles appeared on the same day: January 7th, 2000.

Hospital facing beds crisis as flu cases soar

BY RACHEL ELLIS
HEALTH CORRESPONDENT

Britain's flu outbreak is getting worse.

Daily Express, p7

BLAIR FACES VILLA SLEAZE PROBE

By Patrick O'Flynn
Chief Political Correspondent

Tony Blair was last night facing a probe by Parliament's official sleazebuster over his failure to declare two family holidays in a Tuscan villa.

Daily Express, p2

Boy lama flees across Himalayas to escape Chinese

The teenage head of one of the four great sects of Tibetan Buddhism has escaped from Chinese communist rule to India after a trek through the Himalayas, sources said yesterday.

Daily Telegraph, p1

New boy Gary scores winner and outshoots Des Lynam

BY BEN SUMMERSKILL
MEDIA EDITOR

They thought it was all over for Match of the Day when long-time presenter Des Lynam walked out of the BBC last summer. But his replacement, ex-England football captain Gary Lineker, has boosted the show's audience by more than 20%.

Daily Express, p23

Dome sweet Dome... for the people

NOT a lot of newspaper editors, top businessmen or other VIPs will be visiting the Millennium Dome. So what they think of it doesn't much matter. What is going to decide its success or failure is whether ordinary people enjoy it. And the Mirror's survey shows that they consider it to be a hit.

Daily Mirror, p7

Top of the pups

Pekingese dog Campbell, a 15-month-old from Glasgow, was named pup of the year yesterday at Baby Crufts in London.

Daily Mirror, p11

Kate's Mosstery man
MODEL PUTS ON BOLD FRONT

Thailand is obviously the place to hang out this winter – especially with a new man.

Daily Mirror, p19

POSTIE'S DOWN UNDER BLUNDER

Baffled Bob Farrow couldn't believe his eyes when a Christmas card from pals who live a mile away arrived with a New Zealand post mark.

Daily Star, p23

Hole lotta trouble

Sixty-four residents were evacuated when their homes started to collapse into a hole.

Daily Star, p11

Crimebuster aged just 13
Schoolgirl wages war on crooks

BY MARTIN STOTE

A schoolgirl has stolen a march on criminals by becoming Britain's youngest Neighbourhood Watch co-ordinator.

Emily Webster, 13, decided to act when she was left depressed and troubled by several raids on her home.

She sought help from a victim support group to overcome her fear, and then visited the crime prevention officer at her local police station.

She designed an anti-crime pamphlet, delivered leaflets to residents, and has now been adopted as the co-ordinator for her area.

Emily, who attends Woodrush School in Hollywood, Birmingham, joined the war on crime after one burglary and two attempted break-ins at her home. She is now organising a meeting to launch the Neighbourhood Watch operation and to determine how big a patch to cover.

Her mother Jo said: "The break-in had a terrible effect on Emily. But the help from the victim support group was great and turned her round. She became determined to beat these evil people."

Ian Garrett, manager of Victim Support for South Birmingham said: "Emily was depressed, frightened and withdrawn because of what happened. Now she is confident and outgoing."

Daily Express, p27

BECKHAM SEES RED ONCE MORE

David Beckham was sent off last night in the latest dramatic episode in Manchester United's nightmare trip to South America.

Independent, p1

---

3 ▷ Key features

The writers:
- use wordplay to catch the reader's attention
- vary the order of words in the sentence to create different effects
- write different kinds of article for different purposes

- Which articles are about:
  the British Prime Minister
  the presenter of BBC's *Match of the Day*?
- What has Emily Webster done to make the newspaper call her a 'crimebuster'?
- According to Ian Garrett, how has Emily changed?

4 > Language skills

Word

A **pun** is the use of two words with different meanings but similar sounds to get a humorous effect. Headline writers often include puns in order to catch the reader's attention.

The story about a prize-winning dog was given the headline *Top of the pups*. This is a pun on the television programme title *Top of the Pops*. It encourages us to think about a top-ten listing of dogs.

1 Talk in pairs about these puns from the cuttings. Then write down a brief explanation for each one.

> • *outshoots Des Lynam* • *Dome sweet Dome* • *Kate's Mosstery man* • *Hole lotta trouble* • *Beckham sees red*

Rhyme is the effect you get by using words with the same, or similar, sounds.

2 Write down the headline that uses rhyme for a light-hearted effect.

Spelling

To understand the wordplay in the headline *Hole lotta trouble*, we have to know that *hole* sounds like another word which can be spelt *whole*. W is silent in many common words such as *two*, *who* and *sword*. It is also silent before *-r*.

1 Write down as many *wr-* words that you can think of. (You can begin with the one in the last sentence.)

Sentence

The **subject** of the sentence is the person or thing about which something is said. The **verb** is the word in the sentence which enables us to say what people or things are doing or being.

People who write news stories have to grab the reader's attention and then get their facts across clearly and interestingly. To do this successfully, they begin many of their sentences with the subject followed by the verb. For example:

> *Sixty-four residents* (subject) *were evacuated* (verb) *when...*

1 Reread the article with the headline *Crimebuster aged just 13* and write down five examples of sentences which begin with the subject followed immediately by the verb. You could start by looking at the sentences which begin each of the first three paragraphs.

2 Look back through the other cuttings. Write down five more examples of opening sentences (not the headlines themselves) which begin in the same way, with the subject coming first.

An **adjective** is a word which describes somebody or something. It gives more information about a noun or pronoun. A group of words which does the same job as an adjective is called an **adjectival phrase**.

Often in news reports an adjectival phrase will be added to the subject to provide important information:

Spencer Smith (subject), *the former world triathlon champion* (adjectival phrase), *has turned* (verb) *his back on…*

Sometimes the adjectival phrase is placed in front of the subject:

ex-England football captain (adjectival phrase) *Gary Lineker* (subject) *has boosted the show's audience…*

❸ Which one article has an adjectival phrase at the beginning, with the subject following it?

❹ Here are three adjectival phrases and three subjects with their verbs. Put them together to make the start of three opening sentences, with the adjectival phrase coming first.

Adjectival phrases	Subjects and verbs
Former Olympic gold-medal winner	Sir Paul McCartney believes…
Painter, composer and ex-Beatle	J K Rowling has decided…
Millionaire creator of Harry Potter	Sally Gunnell knows…

❺ Complete the three sentences you have just put together to make up three news items. (For example J K Rowling might have decided to write a new series of books with a different main character.)

❻ Rewrite your three sentences so that the adjectival phrase comes after the subject but before the verb. For example the sentence *Oscar-winning US director Steven Spielberg is to make a new film* would become *Steven Spielberg, the Oscar-winning US director, is to make a new film.*

Text

Newspapers contain many different kinds of **news articles** and reports written about a variety of subjects.

❶ Look at these labels for the many different kinds of news article that a newspaper might contain. Then try to find an example of each one from among the cuttings.

● Political news report

● Sports news report

● Health news report

● International news – a report on something that has happened overseas

● Media news – of interest to readers who watch television and listen to popular music

● 'Leader' article – in which the newspaper expresses its opinions on an important subject, or reports on its readers' views

● Human interest story – something about ordinary people

● Celebrity story – about somebody from the world of sport or entertainment

● Light-hearted story – something amusing and fairly unimportant

5 ▷ Planning your own writing

Invent the headlines and opening sentences of ten different articles which might appear in the same newspaper on the same day.

▶▶ STARTING POINT

The cuttings on pages 8–9 were all from January 7th, 2000. To get some ideas, think about what might be in the news in the future – either in ten days' time or even ten years' time. Then make a list of some of the news reports and feature articles which might appear in those newspapers. For each one, draft an eye-catching headline and the opening sentence. It will help to talk together about possible future events. Think, for example, about what might happen in:

- sport (e.g. *Halifax crushes Barcelona in Euro-Final*)

- science and technology (e.g. *New developments in mobile videophones*)

- popular music, cinema and television (e.g. *Robbie Williams to play Napoleon in Spielberg movie*)

▶▶ CLUES FOR SUCCESS

- Make your headline striking: it might include an example of wordplay such as a pun or the use of rhyme.

- Make your opening sentences clear and interesting: they have to grab the reader's attention.

- Think about the range of different news reports and feature articles that a newspaper might contain.

▶▶ REDRAFTING AND IMPROVING

In groups or in pairs, look closely at your own and other people's first drafts. Make suggestions for improving, editing or adding more detail.

Now think about your own revised version. How can your writing be improved even further? Check that:

- some of the headlines contain puns and other forms of wordplay such as rhyme

- the opening sentences capture people's attention

- you have varied the opening sentences by changing the positions of the subject and adjectival phrase

WRITING FRAMES

Don't forget these possible structures for opening sentences.

	Subject		Verb	
	Robbie Williams		has spoken	for the first time...

• *Some have an adjectival phrase after the subject:*

	Subject	Adjectival phrase	Verb	
	Steve Redgrave,	five-times Olympic gold-medallist,	arrived	at Heathrow earlier today

• *Some have the adjectival phrase before the subject:*

Adjectival phrase	Subject		Verb	
Furious singer	Jennifer Lopez		has banned	her ex-boyfriend...

6 ▷ Looking back

If you want to understand how newspapers are written, it is important to be aware of:

● the language of **headlines**

● the ways in which journalists **structure** their sentences

● the many different kinds of article that newspapers contain

Reporting the news

Daily Mail, Friday, March 24, 2000

Threat

Berg half the size of Wales may go adrift

By **James Chapman**

1 ▶ Purpose

In this unit you will:

- read a news report from a daily newspaper
- learn about the language that journalists use and how they construct reports
- write your own newspaper report

» **Subject links:** *geography, science, media studies*

2 ▶ Opening paragraphs

Iceberg!

This article appeared in the Daily Mail *on March 24th, 2000.*

3 ▶ Key features

The writer:

- gets across the great size of the iceberg in a number of different ways
- uses quotes and reported speech to give the reader first-hand comments
- structures the article so as to capture and maintain the reader's attention

AN ICEBERG half the size of Wales is threatening to break away from Antarctica and start drifting towards some of the world's busiest shipping lanes, scientists warned last night.

The huge slab of ice covers more than 4,000 square miles and at 183 miles long and 22 miles wide will be one of the largest bergs on record in the Southern seas.

Scientists were alerted by satellite pictures which revealed massive fissures around the 900-feet thick chunk.

They believe it is only a matter of time before the block of ice breaks free to become the largest of a string to have separated from the Antarctic ice shelf in recent years.

Once adrift, it will dwarf the 40-mile-long iceberg which broke away in October but melted before hitting any ships.

Scientists are increasingly worried about climate changes across Antarctica where temperatures have risen by 2.5 degrees Centigrade over the past 50 years. Many believe that global warming is melting glacier which has seen five shelves collapse since 1930.

Matthew Lazzara of University of Wisconsin's Antar Meteorological Research Cer which analysed the satellite d said: 'This is a very big iceberg, c to a record, if not a new record not often that you see them of magnitude.'

CHILE ARGENT

Falk

Tierr

Fue

Drake F

S

Ross
Ice
Shelf

# of ice titan

BREAKING LOOSE . . .
THE MONSTER ICEBERG

To scale:
The giant
ice sheet
is half
the size
of Wales

...g could drift
...current
...rds the tip of
... America

Satellite image of ice sheet
183 miles long, 22 miles
wide and 900ft deep which
is breaking away from the
Ross Ice Shelf

He said, once free from the Ross ... shelf, it could travel up to 15 ...iles a day. It will either head ...orth towards Brazil, or be dragged ... deep ocean currents towards ...outh Africa.

The danger would come if it ...ntered warmer seas where it would ... broken up into smaller pieces ...at would pose a far greater hazard ... shipping.

Drifting icebergs can also cause major changes in weather patterns as they move into warmer climates. Temperatures drop by up to five degrees Centigrade and fog forms around the ice.

Dr David Vaughan of the British Antarctic Society in Cambridge, said: 'There's no doubt that this is the birth of a very large iceberg. It is interesting because the Ross ice shelf rarely

produces them. It is probably around 100 years since one broke away.'

However, Dr Vaughan said he was unconvinced that global warming was responsible.

'The big question is how often these icebergs are breaking off,' he said. 'If something of this magnitude was happening every year, then I would start to be worried, but at the moment it is not.'

- How long and how wide is the iceberg, measured in miles?
- Which country is it compared with in size?
- How fast could it move and where might it end up?

4 ❭ Language skills

Word

A word or phrase which means the same, or almost the same, as another word is called a **synonym**.

In this article, the journalist James Chapman wants us to understand just how big and powerful this iceberg is. To avoid repeating the same words to describe its great size, he uses synonyms.

❶ Find these adjectives and adjectival phrases in the article and diagram. Write down the phrase or sentence in which each one appears: *titan, monster, giant, huge, massive, very big, very large*

These words are all synonyms for *big*, but one or two add a different shade of meaning. For example, a *titan* was a huge and mighty god from Greek mythology, so the word helps us to imagine the iceberg's size and power. It might also bring to mind the *Titanic*, the great liner which was sunk by an iceberg.

❷ What does the adjective *monster* add to our impression of the iceberg? (Think about Frankenstein's monster and write down what impression of the iceberg comes to mind.)

Spelling

One of the scientists quoted in the iceberg article is named Vaughan. The *gh* in his name are silent letters.

❶ Write down other words in which the *gh* is silent.

❷ Now add words which have the *ght* combination.

❸ In some words, *gh* can be used to make an 'f' sound. One example is *cough*. Write down some others.

Sentence

Journalists will often use **quotes** from eyewitnesses and specialists, reporting what they said word for word.

❶ Write down the names of the two specialists quoted in this article. Then add notes on:

- where each one works
- what kind of job each one does
- what makes each one a suitable person to say something knowledgeable about icebergs

❷ Write down in your own words the main point that the first specialist makes in his quoted statement.

❸ What is the main point that the second one makes in his?

Text

Journalists have to plan their reports very carefully. First they have to think about the **content** of the article (what it is about and what will go into it), then they plan its **structure** (how it should be put together and what should be in each section).

Content

When journalists are deciding on the content of their reports, they often follow a golden rule known as **the 5 Ws**:

- Who (or what) is involved?
- What happened, or what is going to happen?
- When did it (or will it) happen?
- Where did it (or will it) happen?
- Why did it (or will it) happen?

1 Reread the iceberg article and jot down James Chapman's notes for each W:

- What is involved?
- What has happened (and what might happen)?
- When did it happen (and when might something else happen)?
- Where did it happen (and where else might be affected)?
- Why did it happen (what are the possible reasons)?

Structure

The opening paragraph of a newspaper article is called the **intro**. This section is extremely important: after the headline has caught the reader's attention, it has to capture the reader's interest and make him or her want to read on.

2 Which dramatic and attention-grabbing facts does James Chapman use for his intro to the iceberg report?

3 Pick three really effective intros from the articles in Unit 1 on pages 8–9.

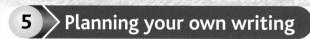

5 ▷ Planning your own writing

Write a newspaper report about something dramatic which has happened or is about to happen.

▶▶ STARTING POINTS

You could write about:

- something which is in the news at the moment – perhaps an environmental disaster like a flood or an earthquake, or the threat of a giant asteroid hitting Earth

- an incident from a book or play you are reading such as the murder of Duncan in Shakespeare's play *Macbeth*

- an incident from history such as the sinking of the *Titanic*

▶▶ CLUES FOR SUCCESS

- Use synonyms to avoid repetition.

- Include quotations from eyewitnesses or specialists.

- Devise an eye-catching headline and a dramatic intro.

- Remember the 5 Ws.

▶▶ REDRAFTING AND IMPROVING

In groups or pairs, look closely at your own and other people's first drafts. Make suggestions for improving, editing or adding more detail.

Now think about your own revised version. How can your writing be improved even further? Check that you have:

- given the report a dramatic intro

- followed the 5W rule

- used synonyms to avoid repetition

- included correctly punctuated quotes

WRITING FRAME

Structure	Make sure you include	Things to remember
Throughout the report	synonyms	the 5 Ws
Headline	eye-catching language	
Intro	dramatic, attention-grabbing facts	
Early paragraphs	important back-up facts	
Middle paragraphs	quotes from an eyewitness or specialist quotes	rules for punctuating
Concluding paragraphs	quotes from a second person	a different viewpoint or opinion?

6 ⟩ Looking back

When you are writing a newspaper report:

- **synonyms** help you to avoid repetition
- **quotes** give the reader first-hand comments and opinions
- well chosen **language** and a carefully planned **structure** will capture and hold the reader's attention

Writing for an audience

Station chase…thief struck as spy was buying ticket at busy Paddington

By JOHN KAY
Chief Reporter

A FRANTIC spy yelled "Stop Thief!" as he chased a crook who had pinched his MI5 computer across a busy station.

The red-faced intelligence agent bawled desperately to cops to help him as he dashed after the agile robber.

Two bobbies on duty at London's Paddington Station scrambled to join in the crazy race through crowds of amazed tube travellers. But the thief – who had grabbed a £2,000 laptop crammed with Government secrets – nimbly dodged and twisted as his three pursuers tried to converge on him.

Report… MI5 chief Stephen Lander

In seconds, with commuters and families staring open-mouthed and stumbling out of his way, he sprinted into a warren of walkways and vanished.

The Keystone Cops2 style caper came after the MI5 "spook" had put down the laptop – full of dossiers on Northern Ireland and other sensitive issues – as he bought a ticket. As he fumbled in his pocket for change, the sharp-eyed opportunist criminal spotted his chance. In a flash he had snatched the bag from beside the agent's feet and hared away.

Embarrassed… the service's HQ

Last night a massive hunt was under way to recover the computer as MI5 squirmed with embarrassment over the latest astonishing security blunder.

A squad of over 150

Special Branch and police officers was trying to locate the computer which was being carried by a middle-ranking operative of MI5, the Government's home intelligence service.

Officials insisted the material stored on the laptop was so well encrypted, or coded, that

1 ▶ Purpose

In this unit you will:

- read a news report from a daily newspaper
- learn about the styles of writing that different newspapers use
- write your own newspaper report in a particular style

» **Subject links:** *ICT, history*

2 ▶ An informal news report

Stop thief!

This article appeared in
The Sun *on March 24th, 2000.*

3 ▶ Key features

The writer:

- uses informal, colloquial expressions
- employs short sentences with simple structures
- divides the article into short paragraphs

THE SUN, Friday, March 24, 2000

N EXCLUSIVE

STOP HIM

MI5 agent's desperate cry as thief grabs laptop with state's top secrets

THIEF'S PRIZE
Opportunist crook swiped £2,000 laptop computer like this from spy

nobody could access or make use of it.

But other experts claimed the code COULD be cracked and feared the secrets would no longer be safe.

And a senior security source admitted: "The theft is extremely regrettable. We want the laptop back."

MI5 director general Stephen Lander has given a full report on the incident to Home Secretary Jack Straw. And Mr Straw in turn has briefed PM Tony Blair, overall head of security services.

RAF MAN'S GOOF

The theft is the most embarrassing security breach since a laptop was nicked from RAF man David Farquhar ten years ago.

The Wing Commander lost his job after the computer containing secrets of the Allies' Gulf War plans was swiped from his official car.

Farquhar had stopped his Vauxhall to visit a car showroom in Acton, West London. A thief smashed windows and pinched the laptop and two briefcases.

- What are we told about the man who had the laptop stolen? Who did he work for? What was his rank?
- What kind of secret material was on the laptop?
- Why might the thief have had difficulty reading it?

4 ⟩ Language skills

Word

When a writer uses a vocabulary and expressions which are closer to everyday, informal speech, we call it **colloquial** language.

This article from the *Sun* newspaper is full of colloquial language. For example, the following words and phrases are more usually found in informal speech than in writing: *pinched, red-faced, cops, bobbies, 'spook', crazy race, hared away.*

❶ Find the sentences in which those words and phrases occur and rewrite them, using formal English. *Cops*, for example, would normally appear as *police officers*.

❷ The article 'RAF man's goof' was printed in the Sun alongside 'Stop him'. Find the examples of colloquial English in both the headline and the article itself. For example, there are three colloquial words for the idea of stealing.

Spelling

Computers are helpful for checking spellings, but some computer language can cause spelling problems.

❶ Use an up-to-date dictionary to check the differences in the meanings and uses of *disc* and *disk*, *programme* and *program*, *bit* and *byte*.

Sentence

Register is the name given to the style of language we choose, to suit a particular situation or a certain kind of subject matter.

There is a difference between *formal register* (used when you are writing a letter applying for a job, for example) and *informal register* (used, say, in a letter written to a close friend). Writing in an informal register will be more colloquial. (Look back at the **Word** section to remind yourself about colloquial language.) Often it will also be more light-hearted. We might say that the 'Stop him' article is in a fairly informal register because it contains colloquial language.

❶ In pairs, read these two extracts from newspaper articles about the passport issued to animals for the first time in February 2000. Which one:

● contains examples of colloquial English? (list the examples)

● is written in a light-hearted way? (find examples of phrases which the writer probably intends to be amusing)

● employs more difficult vocabulary? (list some examples)

● raises serious issues? (name the issue)

When you look at the evidence, which one would you therefore say was in a formal register and which one in an informal one?

a

This is the dramatic proof that the Mirror mutt, Colin the collie, was the first dog to arrive in Britain with a new pet passport.

There was competition from five-year-old Frodo Baggins, whose owner had cheekily paid for a head start. But Colin's Mondeo beat Frodo's BMW by yards to become first back on British soil at 12.30 am yesterday.

Dawn Alford

b

Now at last we have got over our irrational fear of rabies, and all mammals can pass through customs without fear of being caged for six months. All mammals except asylum seekers, that is. So that's why they are abolishing quarantine for pets: they need all the cages for refugees. Afghan hounds are welcome; Afghan people get a bone and a bowl of water and are told to stay away.

John O'Farrell

Text

A **paragraph** is a block of sentences linked by one overall idea or topic.

Newspaper articles often have much shorter paragraphs than you find in books. This helps to keep the reader's attention, which is important when you remember that many people read their newspaper in places such as a crowded bus or a noisy canteen.

The first two paragraphs of the 'Stop him' article are each only one sentence long.

❶ Count how many paragraphs there are in the whole of the article. Then restructure the article so that there are only four paragraphs. Give each one a new topic heading and write down the opening few words of the paragraph. There is a suggestion for the first one, to start you off.

New paragraphs	Opening words	Topic heading
1	*A frantic spy...*	*How the theft happened*
2		
3		
4		

5 ▷ Planning your own writing

Write an article in an informal register about a fairly light-hearted event.

▷▷ STARTING POINTS

The event you are reporting could be:

- something that made somebody look foolish (like the MI5 man having his computer stolen)

- anything to do with animals that isn't depressing (like the introduction of pets' passports)

- anything offbeat

▷▷ CLUES FOR SUCCESS

An article written in an informal register will probably include:

- colloquial language

- simple vocabulary

- short paragraphs

- references to popular culture (such as TV soaps or comedy)

It is also likely to avoid serious issues.

▷▷ WRITING FRAME

Here is an example to start you off. You could either complete the paragraphs begun in the frame, or simply use them as a structure for your own ideas.

Structure	Make sure you include
Throughout the article	• the 5 Ws (see page 17) • colloquial language • varied types of sentence • short paragraphs
Headline	puns and wordplay (see page 10)
Intro	attention-grabbing fact
Paragraph 2	important background fact
Early paragraphs	more details
Middle paragraphs	the rest of the story quotes
	reported speech
Concluding paragraph	a witty comment

Example

(taken from the *Daily Star*, March 24th, 2000)

GOLFER IS BEATEN BLACK AND ROO

Golfer Steve Shorten went to find his ball in the rough... and was grabbed by a KANGAROO

Steve was searching through the long grass when he heard a noise like...

Terrified Steve swung at the angry animal with his driver...

In the appeal court yesterday...
Shocked Steve gasped...
...Summing up, the judge said: 'The club knew of the risk...'
Steve confirmed that he...

The club has now added a warning on its scorecards about the course's unusual handicap. It reads...

REDRAFTING AND IMPROVING

In groups or pairs, look closely at your own and other people's first drafts. Make suggestions for improving, editing or adding more detail.

Now think about your own revised version. How can your writing be improved even further? Check that you have:

- given your article an eye-catching headline

- structured it with an attention-grabbing intro and paragraphs which make the reader want to read on

- included all the features listed in the writing frame

6 ❭ **Looking back**

- Many journalists will employ different registers for different kinds of article.

- Informal register often includes colloquial language.

- To make a newspaper article easier to read, journalists will often write in short paragraphs.

Who needs to advertise?

1 ▷ Purpose

In this unit you will:

- study some advertisements
- learn about the language of advertising, the different organisations who advertise and the places where their advertisements are shown
- plan an advertisement for a charity or campaign

▷▷ **Subject links:** *PSHE, art, graphics, media studies*

2 ▷ Advertisements

Argos, beans and cornflakes: an ABC of advertising

Here is a small sample of the many advertisements that you might see in a single day. They are all trying to sell a 'product'. Many products are things that can be bought in shops – from Coca-Cola to computers – some are services such as banking or holidays. Even charities like the RSPCA think of themselves as selling a 'product'.

I'll be your Valentine

Will you be mine?

Sponsor a dog like me today – and you'll gain a truly loving friend...

That's right, for just £1 a week you can sponsor an abandoned dog like me. You'll be helping the NCDL to give an abandoned dog who may never be rehomed a safe and happy life at one of their 15 Rehoming Centres. You'll also help thousands of other dogs who are cared for by the NCDL every year. In return, you'll get a sponsor's certificate, updates on your dog – and a very faithful friend. So if you want true love for ever, sponsor a dog today.

YES, I'd L♥VE a best friend

☐ Please send me my FREE poster guide so I can choose a dog to sponsor today.
Mr/Mrs/Miss/Ms/Other
Address

Postcode

Please return this form to: Sponsor A Dog, NCDL, FREEPOST LON6996, London E1 8BR. www.ncdl.org.uk
Registered Charity No. 227523   887900

WELCOME TO RESORTS THE PHARAOHS THEMSELVES WOULD HAVE CHOSEN.

Sprinkled along the edge of the Red Sea like so many discarded jewels, the resorts of Egypt's Riviera coastline bask in year-round sunshine.

Warm, white beaches are lapped by clear blue seas. Coral reefs teem with glittering, exotic fish whose colours would shame a rainbow.

Little wonder that the waters off popular resorts like Hurghada and Sharm-el-Sheikh boast some of the most sought-after snorkelling and scuba diving in the world.

Come evening, and there is nightlife aplenty. There are clubs and casinos and international

cuisine to enjoy before you retire to your hotel to dream of the next day's adventures.

Should you tire of the pleasures of the twenty-first century, you could take an excursion to Luxor and the Valley of the Kings, or visit St Catherine's Monastery at the mountain where Moses received the Ten Commandments.

Talk to your travel agent today about the tempting packages we have on offer.

For further information contact The Egyptian State Tourist Authority, Egyptian House, 170 Piccadilly, London, W1V 9DD. **Telephone: 09001 600299** *(Rate 60p/minute)*

'I WISH I WAS IN EGYPT

SINAI AND THE RED SEA RESORTS

3 ⟩ Key features

Advertisers:

- can be all sorts of different people and organisations
- choose words and images carefully to have a particular impact
- advertise in many different places, including magazines, television and the internet

4 Language skills

Word

Advertisers and other writers use **emotive words** when they want to have a particular effect on our feelings and emotions.

The advertisement for holidays in Egypt contains a large number of words which make us feel that Egypt is a place of warmth and beauty.

1 Find these words and phrases. They are all often found in other holiday advertisements.

Paragraph 1:
- an adjective with a noun to make us think that Egypt's seaside resorts are like beautiful, precious objects which most people have forgotten about

- a verb to remind us of lying in the sunshine, soaking it up

Paragraph 2:
- two adjectives to describe the feel and colour of perfect beaches

- a verb to suggest that the waves are gentle and the sea is calm

- an adjective to describe the strange beauty of the fish

Paragraph 3:
- an adjective which lets you know that people come from all over the world because the water-sports are so good

Spelling

The Egypt advertisement contains several examples of **plurals**. The most common way to turn a noun into its plural is simply to add an *s*:

sea – seas   resort – resorts

But words which end in *-ss, -x, -ch* or *-sh* form plurals by adding *-es*:

beach – beaches

1 Think up an example of words ending in these letters and write down their plurals.

2 Write down the rule for nouns ending in *-y* (such as *lady*). How do they form their plurals?

3 Write down the plurals of these nouns: *ox, wolf, sheep*.

Sentence

Advertising **slogans** are short, catchy phrases which are designed to stick in the memory. One of the most famous of all advertising slogans was the extremely simple: *Coke – it's the real thing*. Softees shoes use the slogan the *Soft option*.

❶ Make a list of your favourite advertising slogans. Pick one and explain why you think it is effective.

❷ Invent a slogan to advertise a new product (such as trainers, a chocolate bar or pizza.) Then write a sentence or two to explain your decisions about the language you chose to use.

Text

The different places where advertisements can appear – such as magazines, television or the Internet – are known as advertising **media**. Magazines, newspapers, leaflets and posters all come under the heading of **print** media (because they are printed, rather than shown in moving images, as in television or film).

❶ Here are some examples of the many places where you might see print-media advertisements:

roadside billboards, catalogues, leaflets, magazines, newspapers, posters, T-shirts, wrapping-paper

Where else could you see print-media advertisements? Write your own list. (It will help to imagine your daily journey to school or to the shops. You might walk past buses, for example, or people with supermarket carrier-bags…)

❷ Compare your final list with other people's. It will show you how far you are surrounded by print advertising wherever you go. Where would you say you see the most print advertising (at home; in shops; walking along the street…)?

❸ Create a poster to show a variety of the different places where we see print-media advertising. For example, you might have an illustration of a busy street; there could be a bus queue of people reading different newspapers and magazines; a poster on a billboard; a van driving past…

Most advertisements in magazines, newspapers and leaflets will be a combination of writing, known as **copy**, and a picture, known as the **image**. (The main block of copy is known as the **body copy**.)

❹ Which of the advertisements featured on pages 26–27 has the most copy; and which the least? Why do you think the one with the most has so much?

❺ Which one, in your opinion, has the most eye-catching image? Write down your reasons for choosing it.

5 Planning your own writing

Imagine you have been asked to create a magazine advertisement for a charity or a campaign. Draw up a rough draft of your advertisement.

STARTING POINTS

- You could choose a well-known national charity, such as Oxfam or The Royal Society for the Protection of Birds, or one of the many local charities.

- You might decide on an international campaign (to send aid to people who are starving, for example) or a local one (such as saving woodland from developers or repairing a public building).

- Remember that your charity or campaign is as much a 'product' as Walker's crisps or Warwick Castle.

CLUES FOR SUCCESS

- Look at as many charity and campaign advertisements as you can – they will give you ideas.

- In the early stages, don't spend too much time on the image – simply give a general idea of what it will be. But plan out the copy very carefully.

- Use emotive words to influence the way the reader will feel about your product.

- Think up a memorable slogan.

- Don't make your copy too long, but make sure it covers the most important things you want to say – the points that will help to sell your product.

REDRAFTING AND IMPROVING

Look at your first draft. Check that:

- the copy is interesting and lively enough to catch people's attention

- the copy and image together will persuade people to buy the product

WRITING FRAMES

You may like to follow the design of the dog sponsorship advertisement.

THE EYE-CATCHER
- a well-known saying (*I'll be your Valentine...*) combined with an unexpected image

THE IMAGE
- Valentine hearts
- an appealing photograph of a rather sad dog

THE BODY COPY
- the main point (*Sponsor a dog...*)
  words 'spoken' by the dog
- details (the cost, etc)
  language which addresses the reader directly (*That's right, for just £1 a week you can...*)
  emotive words (*abandoned* contrasted with *truly loving, safe, happy, faithful*)

ATTRACTIVE POINTS
- what you get out of it (*In return, you'll get...*)
- concluding point which reminds us of the Valentine idea (*So if you want true love...*)
  Reply slip (not necessary in advertisements for most products)
  The logo (an eye-catching design which gets across the idea of the organisation)
  The slogan (*A dog is for life*)

---

6 ▷ Looking back

- All sorts of different companies and organisations find it helpful to advertise.

- Advertisements can appear in many different **media**, including print media (such as newspapers and magazines), television and the Internet

- People who design advertisements choose their **words** and **images** with great care.

Selling the product

1 > **Purpose**

In this unit you will:

- study two magazine advertisements for different products
- learn about some special features of print-media advertising
- plan your own print-media advertisement for a commercial product

>> **Subject links:** *PSHE, art, graphics, media studies*

2 > **Advertising in magazines**

Fanta House and Twiglets Treble

These two advertisements both appeared in magazines read by young people.

SHARE iT · LiVE iT

Do you and six mates* want to watch the **latest DVDs**, with full-on cinema sound? To play Nintendo, **pool or pinball** to your heart's content, get out-and-about in the garden or just relax and **chill-out**? Want to eat your favourite snacks and drinks **any time** of day? Or how about recording your own music in the **sound studio**? All this and more, plus a chauffeur-driven **limo** at your disposal? Want it?

WiN iT

For a chance to win one of ten 48-hour stays, call 'Fanta' House on

0845 30 400 30**

Simply choose your preferred visit date and leave your name and details (and those of a parent or guardian if you are under 18 years) by 5pm on **12.05.2000.**

*Two of the seven members of the group must be aged 18 years or over. **Calls will be charged at local rate, please ask the permission of the person who pays the bill before calling.

No purchase necessary. Closing date for receipt of entries is 12.05.2000 by 5pm. Choose one 48-hour stay (2 nights on the following dates: 2-4th June, 16-18th June, 23-25th June, 7-9th July, 14-16th July, 21-23rd July, 24-26th July, 27-29th July, 30th July to 1st August or 2-4th August.) Parental/guardian consent to enter required for entrants under 18 years. The parent/guardian of each winner and guest under 18 years will be sent a formal letter of consent which must be signed and returned to confirm the parent/guardian's agreement to the winner or guest staying at 'Fanta' House. Two of the seven members of the group must be aged 18 years or over. The stay at 'Fanta' House is subject to 'Fanta' House Rules. For full prize details and full terms and conditions please write to: 'Fanta' House Magazine Promotion, Full Terms & Conditions, PO Box 446, St Albans AL4 0YJ. Promoter: Coca-Cola Great Britain, Charter Place, Vine Street, Uxbridge, Middlesex, UB8 1ST. **No promotional correspondence should be sent to this address.** 'Fanta' is a registered trade mark of The Coca-Cola Company.

THE TREBLE'S IN THE BAG

3 Key features

The two advertisers:
- use wordplay to capture our attention and make us think about the product
- choose language which will appeal to the people who might buy the product
- use a clever combination of words and images to sell the product

4 ▶ Language skills

Word

Particular groups of people (for example, teenagers, football fans or computer wizards) often develop their own **special vocabulary**, sometimes known as **jargon**, that other people outside their group will not easily understand.

The body copy of the Fanta advertisement (the six lines from *Do you...* to *Want it?*) contains a number of words and phrases which are most likely to be used by younger people. Some of them are jargon words.

1 How would you explain the following words and phrases? Redraft each one in language that older people might understand.

- *the latest DVDs*
- *full-on cinema sound*
- *Nintendo*
- *chill-out*
- *chauffeur-driven limo*

2 The only copy in the Twiglets advertisement (apart from the words on the packets) is the slogan *The Treble's in the Bag*. *The Treble* can mean the three different flavours available. What else can it mean? Which group of people will most easily understand this other specialist meaning?

Spelling

Puns often depend on **homophones**, words which sound the same, but have different spellings and meanings:

here – hear   there– their– they're

1 Write down the spellings of the words which complete these homophone pairs. The first one has been done to start you off:

*beach/beech   been/   blue/
break/   die/   heel/   made/
pain/   pair/*

2 Pick five of those homophone pairs and write sentences to illustrate their different meanings (ten sentences in all).

Sentence

Advertisements often contain **imperative** sentences: ones which tell you or ask you to do something.

1 Create a series of cartoons to show when and where you might hear these imperatives used:

Keep out!   Get off!   Have a sandwich.   Give us a chance. Please sit down.   Beware of the dog.   Answer the following questions.   Relax in a Radox bath. Explore the Lake District.

Text

When we want to talk about the special kinds of lettering used in advertising and the print media, we use the term **typography** (the study of the way words are typed, drawn or printed).

Look back at the advertisements on page 27. The type in the Yorkie Bar advertisement is designed to look like the lettering on the bar itself, whilst the clock times on the HP Baked Beans advertisement (*7.15 p.m.* etc) look as though they come from a badly printed timetable or schedule.

1 People who design advertisements, posters and notices think very carefully about choosing lettering that suits the message. Look at the Twiglets advertisement. Write a sentence or two to describe the typography of the word *Twiglets* and explain why you think it might have been chosen.

A **logo** is a special symbol which represents a large organisation such as a business, a charity or a college.

2 Find the logos in the advertisements on pages 26–27 for the National Canine Defence League (NCDL), Marwell Zoo, the FA Premier League, K shoes, and on pages 32–33 for Twiglets and Fanta House. Which one do you think is most effective? Write down your reasons. (Which one is most easily recognisable? Which one are you likely to remember?)

The art of putting images and lettering together for a particular effect is called **graphics**.

3 Look at the leaflet advertising Marwell Zoo on page 27. There are very few words on the front cover. But the graphics – the images, typography and logo all added together – present a clear message about the activities and sights to be enjoyed there.

Now look again at the Twiglets advertisement. How do the images succeed in:

- getting across the 'treble' idea
- underlining the football theme
- representing the three trophies which make up the footballing treble
- making the three Twiglets bags stand out?

5 | Planning your own writing

Imagine you are part of an advertising team that has been asked to create a magazine advertisement for a new product aimed at young people. Draft a proposal (a plan or set of suggestions) to bring to the next planning meeting.

- Think up a main idea – the **concept** (like advertising Twiglets Trebles by using the idea of the football 'treble' and showing treble images).

- Plan your idea under clear headings (there are some suggested headings in the writing frame on page 37).

- Include a rough sketch of the finished advertisement as it will look on the page.

≫ STARTING POINT

- Your product might be a new snack, a chocolate bar, or something to do with computers.

- Decide on the outlets – the kinds of magazine in which the advertisement will appear.

≫ CLUES FOR SUCCESS

- Remember that the language and the images should appeal to young people.

- Think up graphics which will help to get the message across.

- Invent a good slogan.

- Think about using imperatives and puns.

≫ REDRAFTING AND IMPROVING

Look at your first draft. Check that:

- it's an exciting and effective way to advertise the product

- you have thought carefully about the language and the graphics

- you have explained your ideas clearly

6 | Looking back

- Print-media advertisers combine **special vocabulary** with **graphics** (typography and images) to sell their products.

- The language often includes **wordplay** and is selected to suit the people at whom the advertisement is aimed.

- Features such as the **typography** and the **logo** help people to identify the product.

WRITING FRAME

You could use this frame, based on a proposal for advertising
Twiglets Trebles, to present your own ideas in writing. Then add
a rough sketch to show what your advertisement might look like.

Ajax
advertising agency

PRODUCT NAME	*Twiglets Trebles*
CONCEPT	*Use the 'treble' idea:* • *present things in threes* • *make people think about the football treble*
TARGET AUDIENCE	*young males (up to 24)*
OUTLETS	*magazines such as Match of the Day*
GRAPHICS:	
■ MAIN IMAGE	*the three different bag covers, matched up with the three football treble trophies*
■ OTHER IMAGES	*blurred images of football crowds and grass in the background*
■ TYPOGRAPHY	*newspaper headline print for the slogan*
■ MAIN COLOURS	*green background (to represent the football pitch); gold for the trophies; Twiglets bags in their normal colours; band at the top in eye-catching orangey-red*
COPY:	
■ BODY COPY	*no body copy or surrounding copy: focus on the slogan and the copy on the bags themselves*
■ SURROUNDING COPY	*None*
■ HIGHLIGHTED TEXT: CAPITALS LARGER PRINT	} *the slogan*
SLOGAN	*The Treble's in the Bag*
LOGO	*the usual Jacob's logo on the bags themselves*
OTHER FEATURES	*the whole advertisement to look as though it has been pasted together like a page in a football fan's album*

TV advertising and comedy

1 ▷ Purpose

In this unit you will:

- study an advertisement made to be shown on television
- learn about some of the things to look for in an advertisement made for television
- analyse your favourite television advertisement

▶▶ **Subject links:** *PSHE, media studies*

2 ▷ Making an advertisement for television

How jammy can you get?

When television film-makers are planning to shoot an advertisement, they will usually draw an outline first. This is called a storyboard, and it shows a sketch of each shot with explanatory comments. Here are seven storyboard frames from a television advertisement for Jammie Dodgers Dips.

Time	Shot 1 (0–1 second)	Shot 2 (1–2 seconds)
Shot	A bank robber, with a stocking over his face, makes his getaway out of Meads bank, clutching a bag.	Blurred, moving shot of a car parked along the kerb.
Sound		FX: bank alarm ringing.

Time	Shot 3	(3–6 seconds)	
Shot	Shot through the front windscreen to the interior of the car. Two policemen are sitting in the front, calmly eating Jammie Dodgers Dips.		Same shot. The robber leaps into the back seat.
Sound			Robber shouting 'Go, go, go!'

Time			
Shot	Same shot. The policemen quietly smile. One of them calmly locks the doors and they carry on eating their Dips.		Same shot. The robber realises where he is, pulls his mask back over his face, and tries to escape – but he is trapped.
Sound			

Time	Shot 4	(7–9 seconds)
Shot	Cut to a volley of Dips biscuits thudding noisily into the centre of a board like arrows into a target. Splodges of jam hit the board beneath the dips, forming the slogan 'How jammy can you get?'
Sound	An official-sounding police message coming over the distorted radio, saying: 'New Jammie Dodgers Dips. How jammy can you get! Over!'

3 ▶ Key features

The television advertisers:
- work out a clear structure for the advertisement
- think carefully about what the viewer will see and hear at any one moment
- often use humour

4 > Media skills

Moving-image media

Films, television, video and many other similar technologies are known as **moving-image media**.

Moving-image media are different in all sorts of ways from print media. For example, if you are creating a magazine advertisement, you have to think about the copy and the graphics. But anybody making a television advertisement – or any other kind of film – has to think about **vision** (what the audience see), **sound** (what they hear) and **timing** (how long each part of the film will take).

❶ *Vision:* look at the storyboard and list the visual details (things that you can see) in the first shot which set up the situation and let you know exactly what is going on.

Sound: write down the sound in the second shot which adds to our understanding of the narrative (the story).

Timing: which shot is held for the longest time? Why? (List the important parts of the narrative that are in that shot.)

❷ *Vision:* Which important detail are we not allowed to see in the second shot? What are we led to believe, because we have not been given enough visual information?

Sound: Explain what is special about the sound of the voice at the end. Why have the advertisers made it sound like that?

Timing: Jot down, in note form, a brief summary of the main events in the narrative. Then check the storyboard and work out roughly how long each event took to show.

Many television advertisements use **humour** to amuse the audience and interest them in the product. The humour can be verbal (coming from the language used) or visual (to do with what the audience can see).

❸ In what ways did these advertisers hope that their Jammie Dodgers advertisement would be:

- visually funny
- verbally funny?

Genre

The different kinds of narrative (such as horror, western or fantasy) are called **genres**. For example, *Alien*, *Star Wars* and *Jurassic Park* all belong to a genre we call science fiction.

① Place each of these films in one of the genres listed below. Then compare your results with those of another student and discuss any differences.

- Films
  Saving Private Ryan
  The Blair Witch Project
  Goldeneye
  ET

- Genres
  science fiction
  action movie
  war
  horror

② In pairs, make a list of other films which could be included in each one of these genres.

Each genre has its own recognisable and typical features. A comedy film or book which mocks the typical features of a particular genre is called a **parody**. For example, the television series *Red Dwarf* is a parody of science fiction movies. Its characters include an alien (the Cat), a robot (Kryten) and a hologram (Rimmer) – all typical features of science fiction movies.

③ Write down some of the typical features of films which belong to these genres. Use the ideas from *Red Dwarf* to start off the first box. Add other genres of your own at the end.

Genre	Typical features
Science fiction	*aliens, robots, holograms...*
Western Action movie Horror War	

④ Which genre is the Jammie Dodgers advertisement a parody of? How can you tell? List the typical features of that genre that you can see in the advertisement.

Spelling

The word **genre** is French, which is why it does not seem to fit English spelling patterns.

① Look up these other words borrowed from other languages. They are all now English words, but they have kept something like their original pronunciations. Check what each one means, which language it comes from and how it is pronounced:

abseil   au pair   bizarre   cliché
coup   fjord   kayak   lager   lasagne

5 ▷ Planning your own writing

Pick your favourite television advertisement which uses humour. First draw up a representation of it in a sequence of storyboard frames with notes added (like the example on pages 38–39). Then write an analysis of the advertisement and say why it is effective, in your opinion.

≫ STARTING POINT

Pick an advertisement that you know well. It will help if you can video it and watch it several times.

≫ CLUES FOR SUCCESS

- When you are writing your analysis, remember to make comments under all three headings: sound, vision and timing.

- Try to define the kind of humour that is being used. Is it verbal humour (relying on puns, for example)? Is it visual humour (like the PG Tips chimpanzees)? Or perhaps it combines both. Is it a parody of a well-known genre (science fiction, perhaps, or westerns)? Or is it based on one particular story or film?

≫ WRITING FRAME

To help you, here is an analysis based on the Jammie Dodgers Dips advertisement.

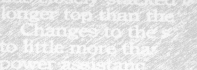

Analysing a television advertisement

Paragraph	Content
1	introduction: the general idea of the ad
2	a brief description of the ad
3	the visual humour
4	the verbal humour
5	sound
6	timing
7	the use of parody
8	conclusion: the overall success of the ad

Some opening phrases

The advertisers have based their ad on the two meanings of the word 'jammy'...

The ad opens with a robber making his escape from Meads Bank...

The expressions on the faces of the bank robber and the two policemen are...

There are very few words heard, but...

The accompanying sounds help to... For example...

Everything happens at a great rush... The longest shot is...

Because we are familiar with the genre...

This ad succeeds because...

>> **REDRAFTING AND IMPROVING**

Reread your analysis. Check that you have:

- focused on details of the advertisement, not only general impressions
- dealt with vision, sound and timing
- explained exactly what type of humour is being used
- decided what makes the advertisement effective

6 > Looking back

- Films, television and cinema are known as **moving-image media**. We study them in different ways from print media.
- Different kinds of narrative are known as **genres**.
- Anything which mocks the features of a genre is called a **parody**.

Match of the day

1 ⟩ Purpose

In this unit you will:
- study an incident filmed for television
- learn how to discuss what you see on a television screen
- plan your own television coverage of a dramatic moment

⟫ Subject links: *PE, history, RE, media studies*

2 ⟩ Capturing a moment on television

Kung-fu Cantona

A few seasons ago Crystal Palace were playing Manchester United. Towards the end of the first half there was an incident involving the Manchester United player, Eric Cantona. Cantona was shown a red card and sent off. Television cameras recorded what happened next.

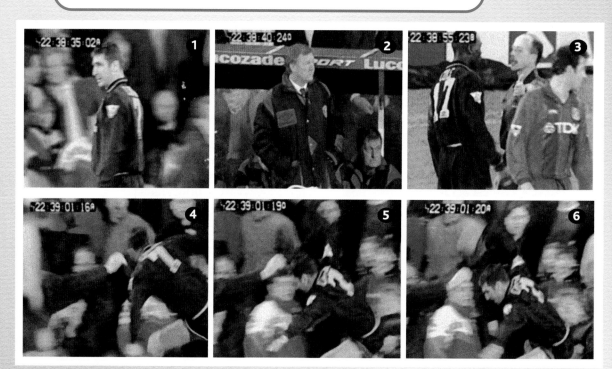

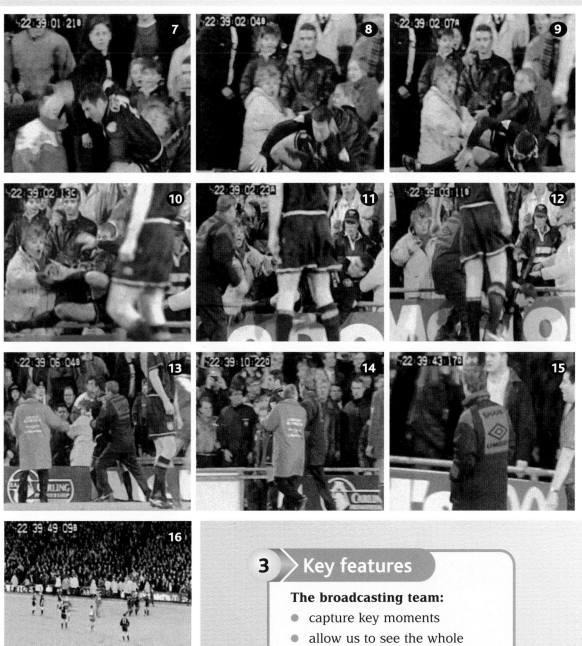

3 ▶ Key features

The broadcasting team:

● capture key moments
● allow us to see the whole of the main incident
● switch cameras to give a view of other people's reactions

4 > Media skills

Moving-image media

Each individual picture on pages 44–45 can be called a **frame**. It is really only films which have frames: if you hold out a strip of film, you can see each individual frame. Television works quite differently – even so, the term 'frame' can still be used to describe each single split-second picture.

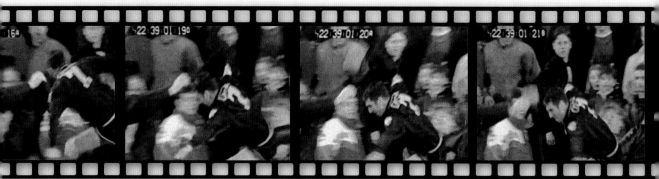

❶ Which frame allows you to see:

- the expression on Cantona's face
- Alex Ferguson's concern at the sending-off
- what Cantona was doing
- the reaction of the crowd nearest to the incident
- the high-point of Cantona's kick
- the officials running to restrain him?

❷ Imagine there had been a camera in the crowd behind the incident, taking shots of the field of play. Draw a sketch of a frame at the moment when Cantona made contact with the abusive fan.

A series of frames which tells part of a story is called a **sequence**. A sequence is like a scene in a play, or an episode in a novel. It tells one part of the whole story and is linked to what comes before it and after it.

❸ Write out the Cantona incident as though it were a section in the middle of a short story. You do not have to set the scene or write a conclusion. Simply start with something like: *Forty minutes into the match, the referee blew for a foul by Cantona...*

A single uninterrupted run of the camera is called a **shot**.

At any one moment in a televised football match, there will be several cameras all taking different shots. For example, there might be several cameras following the ball from different viewpoints above the stands, other cameras placed behind each goal, others taking a shot of the whole field of play, and so on.

4 How many different shots are there in the recording of the Cantona incident?

The job of selecting and joining camera shots is called **editing**. The person in charge of it is the editor.

The editor not only selects the camera shot the viewer should see. He or she also decides how long that particular shot should be held until it is time to switch to another one. If you hold a shot too long, the viewer gets bored and might also miss some important action on another camera; switch cameras too often and it all gets very messy and disjointed.

5 The longest shot in this sequence is shown in frames 4 to 14. How long does the editor decide to hold that shot? (Check the timings in the top-left of each frame.) Why do you think the editor decides not to change camera shots during this time?

6 Imagine you had been the editor of this programme and were being interviewed afterwards. How might you have answered the following questions? Write out the editor's replies.

> INTERVIEWER *After Cantona's booking, you had a good shot of him walking off (frame 1). Why did you switch cameras to show other shots (frames 2 and 3)? What were you interested in?*

> EDITOR...

> INTERVIEWER *Why did you decide to keep the camera on Alex Ferguson after the incident (frame 15)?*

> EDITOR ...

> INTERVIEWER *Why did you show that long shot of the players at the end (frame 16)?*

> EDITOR ...

7 Write down any other things that the editor might want to say about this sequence. What was he or she most satisfied with? What might have been done better?

5 ▷ Planning your own writing

Pick a famous historic moment from before the days of television (in other words, earlier than the 1920s). Now imagine that television had been invented and that you were editing a live broadcast. You have four cameras in good positions, ready to record the incident.

- Sketch a sequence of frames to represent what the viewers would have seen in any two-minute spell.

- Add a brief caption below each frame to help describe what we are seeing.

- Finally, write a short account to explain your decisions.

▷▷ STARTING POINTS

- Pick a really dramatic moment in history when there would have been something exciting to see. It might be easiest to use an event that you have been learning about in history lessons.

- Alternatively, you might choose the moment when:

  King Harold's army is attacked at the Battle of Hastings in 1066 and he gets an arrow in his eye

  London goes up in flames during the Great Fire of 1666

  Nelson is killed at the Battle of Trafalgar, 1805

  Emmeline Pankhurst's suffragettes smash windows demonstrating about votes for women in 1905

  soldiers go over the top in the Battle of the Somme in 1916

- Before you start, do some research in history books or on the Internet to find out in detail what happened.

▷▷ MEDIA FRAME

To give you some ideas, here are the first six frames for a famous moment in history. It is 1649 and King Charles I is about to have his head chopped off…

▷▷ CLUES FOR SUCCESS

- Make sure that your frames make up a sequence: a complete scene in the longer story.

- Think carefully about the shots. What are the best positions for your cameras? Before you start, draw a sketch-plan of the scene.

- Remember that it is your job as editor to make decisions each moment about which camera shot to take.

- You also have to decide how long each shot should last before switching to another camera. (Check how long the whole Cantona kick took – see question 5 on page 47.) Write in the timings in seconds only. Start at 00 seconds and then show the time of each frame, through to about two minutes (02.00).

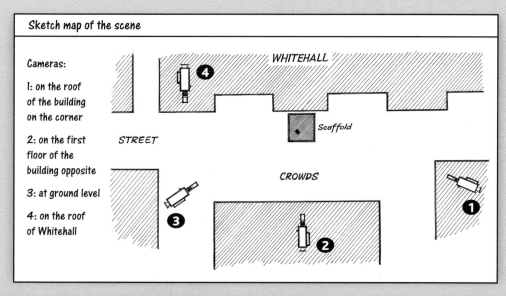

00 secs	02 secs	05 secs	10 secs	13 secs	18 secs
Camera 1	Camera 2	Camera 3	Camera 4	Camera 4	Camera 2
A roof-top view of Whitehall and the area outside	The window in Whitehall through which the King is expected to appear	The crowd	Members of parliament arriving to witness the execution	The members of parliament take their places	Some movement behind the window

---

►► REDRAFTING AND IMPROVING

Look back at your sketches. Check that you have:

- allowed viewers to see all the most interesting moments
- set up a good variety of different shots
- timed each shot carefully (not too long so that viewers become bored; not too short so that the whole thing becomes disjointed)

6 ▷ Looking back

- A picture of a single moment of a film, video or television recording is called a **frame**.

- A **sequence** is a section of a film or broadcast which tells part of the complete story.

- A **shot** is a single view through a camera.

- The job of selecting and switching from one camera shot to another is called **editing**.

Screen horror

1 Purpose

In this unit you will:
- study a sequence from a film
- learn about some of the things to look for in a film
- create your own storyboard

>> **Subject links:** *history, art, English literature, media studies*

2 Studying a film

Frankenstein

There have been many films made of Mary Shelley's famous novel Frankenstein, *and they all tell the story slightly differently. This is one version, represented in a storyboard (a drawing of the sequence of shots).*

Victor Frankenstein has created a monstrous creature from human body parts. But the monster has escaped and, having killed Frankenstein's brother, friend and bride, has fled to the frozen wastes of the Arctic with Frankenstein in pursuit. Frankenstein is discovered on an ice-floe by the crew of an Arctic ship captained by a fanatical explorer called Walton who is driving his men to discover a passage to the North Pole. Worn out by his pursuit, Frankenstein tells Walton his horrifying story and dies.

Shortly afterwards Walton returns to his cabin to find the monster standing over Frankenstein's coffin.

Time	1 hr 56 mins 35 secs	1.56.38
Shot	Medium-shot: monster standing over the coffin	Full-shot: the monster walks around the coffin
Sound	Music throughout the sequence	

Time	1.56.44	1.56.48
Shot	Distant-shot from at sea: an ice-floe with the ship in the background	Close-up: Walton watches the monster
Sound		

3 Key features

The team making the film have:
- used different shots
- planned how the image should be placed in the frame
- cut from one shot to another to achieve effects

6.50	1.56.56	1.56.58	1.57.00	1.57.01
5	**6**	**7**	**8**	**9**
dium-shot: the monster ntly caresses the coffin	Close-up: the monster's face, full of sadness	Close-up: Walton looks down, himself saddened by the sight	Extreme close-up: The monster looks up and sees Walton for the first time	Close-up: Walton's face, wondering what the monster is about to do
sic throughout the sequence				

7.02	1.57.03	1.57.04	1.57.09	1.57.12
10	**11**	**12**	**13**	**14**
reme close-up: the camera ves in to an extreme se-up on Walton's anxious e as he realises	Medium-shot: the monster jumps onto the ledge beneath the cabin window	Close-shot: the two crew members have joined Walton at the door as he shouts to the monster, 'Stay!'	Distant-shot: the ship seen from the sea, with the ice-floe now near to it	Medium-shot: the saddened monster takes a final look down at the coffin

7.26	1.57.36	1.57.40	1.57.49	1.57.54
15	**16**	**17**	**18**	**19**
dium-shot: Captain Walton d the two crew members	Long-shot: the monster, from out at sea, as he leaps from the ship onto the ice-floe	Close-up: the captain looking from the cabin window down onto the ice-floe	Distant-shot: the monster on the ice-floe, seen from the ship	Distant-shot: the ship moves away from the ice-floe

7.58	1.58.01	1.58.04	1.58.10	1.58.13–1.58.20
20	**21**	**22**	**23**	**24**
tant-shot: the ice-floe en from the ship, now ther away	Distant-shot: stern view of the ship sailing away	Same shot as 20, but with the ice-floe now further away	Distant-shot: the ship further away, with the horizon visible behind it	Same shot as 20, the ice-floe now in the distance; the screen fades to black

51

4 > Media skills

Moving-image skills

When you are filming a scene, you can choose from a variety of different **camera shots**. For example, you can have close-ups, where the camera is very near to the subject, or long-shots, taken from further away.

Below are seven frames from *Frankenstein*, showing some of the different shots that the camera can take.

1 Look at the shots used in the final sequence of the film on pages 50–51 and write down some answers to the following questions. Use examples from the sequence to help make your points.

- What can you show the audience with a close-up or extreme close-up that can't be achieved with other shots?

- What can you achieve with a distant-shot?

- What kind of shot is useful for showing two or three people's expressions in a single frame?

- What kind of shot does this director use most often after the monster has leapt onto the ice-floe (frames 16–24)? Why does he use that shot so frequently at that point?

The skill of placing people or objects in a particular place within the edges of the film frame is called **framing**.

Directors use framing to achieve particular effects. For example, this director adds to the tension of the dramatic moment before the monster jumps, by letting Walton's anxious face fill the whole frame.

Close-up

Extreme close-up

Close-shot

Medium-shot

Full-shot

Long-shot

Distant-shot

2 Write down how the framing helps to show:

- the position of the ice-floe in relation to the ship (frame 3)
- Walton's feelings as the monster is about to jump (frame 10)
- the monster's feelings towards the dead Frankenstein (frame 14)
- the loneliness of the monster's death (frame 24)

Changing from one shot to another is called **cutting**. This director cuts from a shot of Walton and his men (frame 15) to a shot of the monster leaping onto the ice-floe (frame 16).

3 How does the cutting help to show the captain's and the monster's emotions at the point where the monster is about to leap out of the window (frames 7–10)?

The skill of joining shots together to get a particular effect is called **montage** (a French word, pronounced *mont-arge*).

4 In the final seven frames (18–24), the director shows only two images. What are they? Write down what you notice about the montage. (Look at the order in which the images are shown.) How does the montage help to show that the monster is now totally alone?

Genre

The different kinds of films with their own special features (such as horror, western, science fiction) are called **genres** (another word borrowed from French). Each different genre can be recognised by typical features. For example, science fiction films normally involve aliens (often trying to conquer the universe), distant planets and amazing futuristic technology.

5 *Frankenstein* and *Dracula* are famous examples of the genre we call horror. Make a table like this and write down some of the typical features of horror films in the right-hand column. To give you an example, the first column has been filled in for one of the best known of all film genres, westerns.

Typical...	Westerns	Horror films
characters	*sheriffs, 'cowboys and Indians', 'baddies', ranchers*	
settings	*the wide-open spaces in America, canyons and gulches, run-down timber-built towns*	
costumes	*ten-gallon hats, spurs, holsters*	
happenings	*gun-fights, pursuits on horseback, saloon brawls, wagon-trains attacked by 'Indians'*	
stories	*good-guys help the weak to defeat the bad-guys*	
examples of language	*'Make your play, Sheriff.'*	

5 ▸ Planning your own writing

Imagine you are making a new film in a well-known genre. Draft a plan in note form of a 30-second sequence (for example, you could choose the moment in a science fiction movie when they first see the aliens). Then draw a storyboard to represent what the audience will see. The frames should be set out like the ones on pages 50–51 and include:

- the timing
- a sketch of what the screen will show
- written notes explaining the shot
- details of the sound, music or dialogue

▸▸ STARTING POINT

- Think up a new story, but include some typical features of the genre that you have chosen.

- Your 30-second sequence can come from anywhere in the film.

- Don't include too much dialogue: in the dramatic *Frankenstein* sequence only one word is spoken.

▸▸ CLUES FOR SUCCESS

Remember some of the skills of filming:

- Use a variety of shots to help tell the story clearly. Think about the different uses of close-ups and distant-shots, for example.

- Framing helps you to focus the audience's attention. In some shots you might want a face or an object to fill the frame.

- Think about montage. The way you cut shots together has a powerful effect. For example, you might keep on cutting from a dramatic incident to an onlooker's face and back again.

▸▸ REDRAFTING AND IMPROVING

Look back at your storyboard. Check that you have:

- included typical features of the genre

- used different shots, framing, montage and sound to tell the story clearly and get ideas across to the audience

MOVING IMAGE FRAMES

Here are four frames from a western, with notes on the director's decisions. You could use the ideas on genre, shots, framing, montage and sound as a basis for your own storyboard. This is the point in the film where the sheriff has challenged the 'bad-guy' to a gunfight in the main street at noon…

Timing	1.25.00	1.25.03	1.25.05	1.25.08
Image				
Typical feature of the genre	The on-lookers run for cover and close up their shops.	The sheriff, good-looking in a rugged sort of way, squints into the sun.	Wind blows dry tumbleweed across the dusty street.	He flexes his hand muscles over the gun.
Shot	Distant-shot of the street, taken from behind the sheriff.	Close-up of his face: tough and determined	The same distant-shot of the street: this is what the sheriff sees	Close-up of his hand poised over his gun.
Framing	Sheriff to one side; the main street fills the rest of the frame.	His face fills the whole frame so that we get a clear idea of his emotions.	The buildings are to the side of the frame, showing how wide and empty the street is.	The hand and gun are to one side, leaving room for us to look down the empty street.
Montage	Cut from the empty street to the sheriff's face, then back to the street, then to his hand over the gun. This builds up the suspense: we see the scene from his viewpoint and share his tension as he waits for the gunman to appear.			
Sound	Dramatic music starts.	Music becomes more tense.	Behind the music is the sound of a heartbeat.	The music suddenly stops. Silence except for the sound of the wind blowing.

6 ▶ Looking back

- Film-makers will have a particular purpose, or range of purposes, in mind when they are filming a sequence.

- A variety of **shots** is used to focus on different things. Close-ups can show things in detail; distant-shots give a wide view of a scene.

- **Framing** helps the director to achieve particular effects. A face might fill the frame to show a person's emotions, or be placed to one side so that other things can be seen at the same time.

- **Montage** is the technique of cutting from one scene to another. It is one of the most important tools the film-maker has for telling a story and creating particular effects.

Shakespeare in action

1 ▶ Purpose

In this unit you will:

- learn how to discuss Shakespeare on film
- understand what people mean by an interpretation of Shakespeare
- analyse the opening of a film version of *Macbeth*

▶▶ **Subject links:** *history, art, English literature, media studies*

2 ▶ Shakespeare – script to screen

Macbeth and the witches

Macbeth has several times been made into a film. Here are frames from the opening of one of them.

Time	00.00	00.15	00.35	00.40
Shot	Dusk. A distant castle silhouetted on a craggy moorland landscape. Rooks wheel around above.	A wooden wedge being hammered into the ground to help support a sturdy, roughly hewn pole.	As the camera holds the shot, looking down at the base of the pole, three pairs of raggedly clothed feet enter the frame.	The camera pans upwards to reveal an old woman (W1) and two younger ones (W2 and W3), staring upwards.
Sound or dialogue	Distant eerie sounds of the rooks and a faint rhythmic hammering sound.	The hammering sound, but louder.	The hammering stops.	

3 ▶ Key features

The writer:

- made some changes to Shakespeare's script
- created strong visual images and sounds
- used props, costumes and make-up to help gain the effect wanted

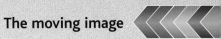
Time	00.45	01.05	01.13	01.30
	❺ THE TRAITOR MACDONWALD	**❻**	**❼**	**❽**
Shot	The camera moves up the pole to take in a crudely drawn notice, held in place by a nail: 'The traitor Macdonwald'.	Cut to a close-up of a severed head, fixed to the top of the pole.	Cut back to the three women, still staring at the head.	The old woman watches one of the younger ones take a jar out of her sack.
Sound or dialogue				

Time	01.30	01.40	01.45	01.50
	❾	**❿**	**⓫**	**⓬**
Shot	The camera pulls down to show the blood staining the sand, as it drips from the severed head.	The three women's heads framed.	One of the younger women (W2), to the left of the frame.	A shot of all three turning back to look at the head on the pole.
Sound or dialogue	All three: *Fair is foul and foul is fair...*	*...Hover through the fog and filthy air.*	W2: *When shall we three meet again? In thunder, lightning, or in rain?*	W1: *When the hurly-burly's done, when the battle's lost, and won.* W2: *That will be ere the set of sun.*

Time	02.00	02.10	02.50	02.55
	⓭	**⓮**	**⓯**	**⓰** MACBETH
Shot	The first two women silhouetted, with the pole between them.	They all trudge off in the direction of the castle.	As they recede, they go out of focus, leaving the head in focus.	The title appears over the image of the head.
Sound or dialogue	W1: *Where the place?* W2: *Upon the heath.* W3: *There to meet with Macbeth.*	Eerie sounds of rooks start up again and continue.		

4 Media skills

Moving-image media

As you learned in Unit 8 (pages 50–55), when you are filming a scene, you can choose from a variety of different **camera shots**. For example, you can have close-ups, where the camera is very near to the subject, or long-shots, taken from further away.

1 Look back at the shots in the storyboard of the film of *Macbeth* on pages 56–57. Make a table like this and fill it in, showing where different types of shots have been used. For example, because frame 1 is a distant-shot, write a 1 in the right-hand box.

Shots	Close-up	Close-shot	Medium-shot	Full-shot	Long-shot	Distant-shot
Frames						1

2 Which kind of shot does the director use most often? Why do you think he makes that choice? What effect does it have?

3 Write down why you think the director chose the particular shot that he did for frame 4.

As you learned in Unit 8 (pages 50–55), the technique of placing people or objects in a particular position within the frame is called **framing**.

This director has thought carefully about how the witches and the objects they use are to be framed. For example, he gains a powerful impact by letting the head almost fill the screen in frame 6.

4 How does he create a sense of mystery with the framing in shot 2?

5 How does the framing in shot 12 fit the dialogue?

6 Pick another shot and write down what you notice about the framing. How does it help to get a particular impression across?

The camera can also take shots from different directions and different heights, such as looking up at an object or viewing it from above. These views are called **camera angles**.

7 What effect does the camera angle have in frames 3 and 9?

Interpretation

An **interpretation** of a play is somebody's idea about what it means. We say that a director or an actor is interpreting a script by performing it in certain ways and making the audience notice particular things.

People interpret Shakespeare's scripts in different ways because they see different meanings in them. For example, one interpretation of the character of Macbeth is that he is already an evil man when the story starts. A quite different interpretation says that he is not a bad man – simply weak – and it is the witches who make him do wicked things.

1 Which of these two interpretations does this director prefer, do you think? How can you tell from the opening of his film version? (Which characters does he focus on? Who seems to have the power at the beginning of the film?)

Location, props and **costumes** all help to get a particular interpretation across.

2 The location is the place in which the scene is filmed. Look at the first shot and find five adjectives to describe the location that the director has chosen. For example, you could start with *isolated*.

3 The word *props* is short for properties – it means all the objects used in a play, from cups and saucers to swords and shields.

How does the jar in frame 8 add to the sinister atmosphere? What are we supposed to think it will be used for?

4 What are the costumes telling us about these women? Are they rich or poor, for example? Are they modern 21st-century women, or do they come from the distant past?

The choice of actors to play particular parts is called **casting**. Sometimes directors will cast actors because of their appearance.

5 How important is the appearance of the three actors playing the witches?

6 What is the effect of having one witch played as a blind person?

7 Shakespeare doesn't give us any clue about the witches' ages. If you were filming *Macbeth*, how old would you make the witches? Why? Would they all be the same age?

5 ▶ Planning your own writing

Write an analysis of the opening sequence of this film version of *Macbeth* to show how the director interprets Shakespeare's script. (The first scene of Shakespeare's *Macbeth* is printed in the Teacher's Portfolio.)

▶▶ STARTING POINT

Think about the ways in which the opening of the film tells us that the story will be:

- scary
- to do with the supernatural
- violent

▶▶ CLUES FOR SUCCESS

- Remember the techniques that film-makers use. They include:

  the camera: camera angles, cutting, montage, framing, varying shots, lighting

  sound: sound effects, music

  location, props and costumes

- Think about the following questions:

  What differences are there between the film script (known as the *screenplay*) and Shakespeare's original script?

  What effect do the changes to the dialogue have?

  Shakespeare calls his characters First, Second and Third Witch. How can a director manage to make them three distinct characters? Think about their physical appearance, their ages, their costume and other features which help to distinguish them.

▶▶ WRITING FRAME

This writing frame shows you how to structure your analysis in seven paragraphs. Each of the central paragraphs (2–6) has the same structure. Take paragraph 3 as an example:

- state your main point (how the opening of the film brings out the supernatural elements)
- explain it with supporting details (it shows witches, magic spells and prophecies)
- back it up with evidence (refer to shot 4 and shots 5–7 – e.g. inscription, the severed head)

How many seconds of the film have passed before the first lines of the script are spoken? What important things have happened before that moment? What powerful impressions have we already received before we hear any of Shakespeare's words?

Look at the shots in which the dialogue is spoken (frames 9–13). Compare the framing of the characters in shot 10 with the framing in shot 13. How do these different choices of framing fit the dialogue?

The witches link the spell with the name of Macbeth: how does the choice of the props they use (such as the severed head) help us to predict the kind of thing that is going to happen to him?

The witches inform us that *Fair is foul and foul is fair*. How do the opening three minutes get across the impression of *foulness*?

Analysing the film of *Macbeth*

Paragraph	Main points	Supporting details	Shot
1	Introduction: the first three minutes establish the story and the atmosphere	Where is this happening? Who are these three strange women? What are they doing?	
2	Setting up the **scary** elements of the story	Eerie bird noises and a disturbing setting The hammer and wedge appears first The frightening physical appearance of the witches	1 2 4
3	Letting us know that this is a story about the **supernatural**	The three women are witches They are casting a spell	4 5–9
4	Introducing the idea that it will be about **violence**	The inscription The severed head The blood	5 6 6, 7,
5	The images match up with Shakespeare's **language**	*...fog and filthy air* *When shall we three meet again...?* *There to meet with Macbeth*	10 11 13
6	Other things that you have noticed		
7	Conclusion: how effective is this as an opening to the film?		

 REDRAFTING AND IMPROVING

Read through your first draft. Check that you have:

- expressed your ideas clearly
- created a clear structure for your analysis
- given examples for each of the points that you make

6 ▷ Looking back

- An **interpretation** of a play is somebody's idea about what it means.

- There are many factors which influence a particular interpretation. They include **camera-work**, editing and the use of sound as well as the choice of **location**, **props**, **costumes** and **casting**.

- This means that when a Shakespeare script is turned into a film, a number of people influence the interpretation. They include not only the director, but also the editor, the actors and the whole production and technical crew.

Book, theatre, radio and cinema

1 ▷ Purpose

In this unit you will:

- see how a novel can be adapted for stage, radio and film
- learn some of the skills needed for work in each of those three media
- write some adaptations of your own

» **Subject links:** *English literature, media studies*

2 ▷ Adapting a novel for different media

The Hound of the Baskervilles

This episode is taken from the middle of Sir Arthur Conan Doyle's famous thriller. Doctor Watson, friend of the detective Sherlock Holmes, is staying with Sir Henry Baskerville in Baskerville Hall, a remote house in the middle of Dartmoor. Holmes fears that Sir Henry's life might be in danger and has sent Watson down to the Hall to act as Sir Henry's bodyguard. Suspicious of the butler, Barrymore, Watson and Sir Henry stay up one night to keep watch on him. Nothing happens on the first night, but they decide to give it one more chance. Several hours pass, and they are beginning to feel that they are wasting their time...

The novel

One struck, and two, and we had almost for the second time given it up in despair, when in an instant we both sat bolt upright in our chairs, with all our weary senses on the alert once more. We had heard the creak of a step in the passage.

Very stealthily we heard it pass along until it died away in the distance. Then the **baronet** gently opened his door, and we set out in pursuit. Already our man had gone round the gallery, and the corridor was all in darkness. Softly we stole along until we had come into the other wing. We were just in time to catch a glimpse of the tall, black-bearded figure, his shoulders rounded, as he tip-toed down the passage. Then he passed through the same door as before, and the light of the candle framed it in the darkness and shot one single yellow beam across the gloom of the corridor. We shuffled cautiously towards it, trying every plank before we dared to put our whole weight upon it. We had taken the precaution of leaving our boots behind us, but even so, the old boards snapped and creaked beneath our tread. Sometimes it seemed impossible that he should fail to hear our approach. However, the man is fortunately rather deaf, and he was entirely preoccupied in that which he was doing. When at last we reached the door and peeped through, we found him crouching at the window, candle in hand, his white intent face pressed against the pane, exactly as I had seen him two nights before.

We had arranged no plan of campaign, but the baronet is a man to whom the most direct way is always the most natural. He walked into the room, and as he did so, Barrymore sprang up from the window with a sharp hiss of his breath, and stood, **livid** and trembling, before us. His dark eyes, glaring out of the white mask of his face, were full of horror and astonishment as he gazed from Sir Henry to me.

'What are you doing here, Barrymore?'

Arthur Conan Doyle

baronet *nobleman (Sir Henry)*

livid *pale*

A stage dramatisation

This is a version of the same episode, adapted for performing on stage.

Act 2, Scene 16

*Baskerville Hall.
A downstairs clock
strikes two, there is
the unmistakable
sound of a creaking
stair, and Barrymore
enters furtively
through a door up
L, carrying a candle.
He walks across the
stage to down R and
then kneels, looking
out at the audience,
as though through a
window, pressing his
face to the pane.*

*There is a long
silence, as Barrymore
peers outwards.*

*Then, as he lifts the
light to the window,
Sir Henry enters from
the same door, and
moves silently up C,
followed by Watson.*

Sir Henry (*sharply*)
What are you doing
here, Barrymore?

*Startled, Barrymore
swings round to face
Sir Henry.*

A radio adaptation

*Here is the radio script for the same moments.
The initials FX stand for sound effects.*

[*FX: clock strikes two.*]

Sir Henry (*despondently*): No luck, Watson. We'll just have to –

Watson Listen!

[*Silence. Then –
FX: creaking floorboards.*]

Sir Henry (*whispering*) It's him!

[*FX: slow, soft footsteps and occasional creaks.*]

Watson (*whispering*) Wait until he passes the door… [*Pause.*] All right – now!

[*FX: door opening quietly. From now on, all the communication
between Watson and Sir Henry is in muffled whispers.*]

Sir Henry He must have turned down into the gallery.

Watson Yes. If I'm right, he'll be in the same room as before.
Come on. He won't be expecting us.

[*FX: Sounds of the two men walking quietly along the gallery:
soft footsteps and rustling clothing.*]

As I thought: there's a light coming from the same room as before. See?

Sir Henry (*sighs*): You're right. I'm going to take a look.

Watson He'll hear you approaching. These boards –

Sir Henry No. His hearing isn't good. Anyway, Watson, I have to know
what he's up to.

Watson All right. But take care. I'll be at your shoulder.

[*FX: More muffled sounds of their movement along the gallery.
A door-hinge groans slightly.*]

What can you see?

Sir Henry It's as you said. He's crouching at the window with a lighted candle.
I'm going in.

Watson No, wait!

[*FX: a door handle being rattled and a door
swung open, followed by determined footsteps.*]

Sir Henry What are you doing here, Barrymore?

A film version

Finally, here is the screenplay of a film version. A screenplay is simply a film script. But it looks different from a stage script because most of it is taken up with camera instructions, rather than dialogue. INT. and EXT. stand for interior (inside) and exterior (outside) shots. Look back at page 52 to check what C.U., M.S. and the other abbreviations stand for.

INT. C.U. OF A CLOCK. IT STRIKES TWO.   141

         CUT TO

INT. M.S. OF WATSON AND SIR HENRY SLUMPED IN THEIR ARMCHAIRS.   142
WATSON SIGHS AND SHAKES HIS HEAD.

         CUT TO

INT. C.U. OF SIR HENRY'S FACE. HE IS FED UP.   143

         CUT TO

INT. L.S. WATSON GETS UP AND TAKES HIS JACKET OFF THE BACK   144
OF HIS CHAIR. SUDDENLY BOTH MEN FREEZE.

         CUT TO

INT. C.U. OF SIR HENRY'S FACE, LOOKING UP EXCITEDLY.   145
FLOORBOARDS CREAK.

         CUT TO

INT. C.U. BARRYMORE'S FEET, AS HE WALKS SILENTLY ALONG   146
THE CORRIDOR.

         CUT TO

INT. C.S. OF WATSON AND SIR HENRY.   147

       WATSON
       Come on!

         CUT TO

INT. L.S. OF THE CORRIDOR. BARRYMORE TURNS A CORNER AT THE END.   148
SIR HENRY COMES INTO FRAME.

         CUT TO

INT. L.S. OF THE GALLERY. BARRYMORE LOOKS FURTIVELY OVER HIS   149
SHOULDER BEFORE PUTTING HIS HAND ON A DOORKNOB.

         CUT TO

INT. M.S. OF THE CORRIDOR. WATSON AND SIR HENRY PEEP ROUND   150
THE CORNER.

CUT TO

INT. M.S. OF THE ROOM. BARRYMORE IS CROUCHING BY THE WINDOW.   151
HE LIGHTS A CANDLE.

CUT TO

EXT. M.S. OF BARRYMORE THROUGH THE WINDOW FROM OUTSIDE.   152
HE RUBS AT THE PANE AND PEERS OUT INTO THE DARKNESS.

CUT TO

INT. L.S. OF THE ROOM FROM BEHIND BARRYMORE.   153

CUT TO

EXT. D.S OF THE MOOR. CRAGGY TORS ARE SILHOUETTED AGAINST   154
A MOONLIT SKY.

CUT TO

INT. M.S BARRYMORE HOLDS THE CANDLE UP TO THE WINDOW   155
AND MOVES IT FROM SIDE TO SIDE.

CUT TO

INT. C.S. OF WATSON AND SIR HENRY WATCHING THROUGH THE   156
PARTLY OPENED DOOR.

CUT TO

INT. C.S. BEHIND BARRYMORE. STARTLED, HE SWINGS ROUND TO   157
THE CAMERA AS HE HEARS SIR HENRY'S VOICE.

SIR HENRY

What are you doing here, Barrymore?

CUT TO

INT. C.U. BARRYMORE'S TERRIFIED FACE.   158

3 > Key features

The three acting versions all tell the story of the novel, but in different ways:

- the stage dramatist has to use a small physical space to represent different locations
- the radio playwright depends upon sound effects and dialogue to let the audience know what is going on
- the film-maker chooses images to let us see what is happening

4 Media skills

Stage dramatisation

As you learned in Unit 9 (pages 56–61), **location** is the name given to the place where a scene happens.

A stage dramatisation has to take place in a particular space. Usually it will not be possible to show characters moving through different parts of the same house, which is what happens in this part of the story.

1 Reread the novel extract and write down the different parts of the house through which Barrymore moves, followed by Watson and Sir Henry.

2 Now look at the stage adaptation. Describe what the dramatist has done to deal with the problem of the different locations.

3 Imagine you were a member of the audience. Draw a rough sketch to represent what you would see at the

moment when Barrymore is shining the light through the window. As well as Barrymore himself, show Sir Henry, Watson and the door.

Stage directions are information given to people performing the play to help them to understand how it can be acted.

4 Look back at the stage adaptation and find an example of each of these four uses for stage directions:

- to set the scene at the beginning
- to mark when silences occur
- to show what the character is doing, or what other things are happening on stage
- to give the actor an idea of how they might say a line

DOWN
STAGE
LEFT
CENTRE
RIGHT
UP
STAGE

Radio adaptation

A radio play has to use **sound effects** and **dialogue** to let the listener know what is happening.

1 Reread the novel extract and the radio adaptation. Pick three sound effects and explain how they help us to understand what is happening in the story. Then find the moment in the novel which is represented by the sound effect. For example, you might write:

> *[FX: clock strikes two.]*
>
> *This shows us how long the men have been waiting.*
>
> *The novel says: 'One struck, and two…'*

2 Now pick three examples from the dialogue which help us to understand what is going on. Again, find the moment in the novel which is represented by the dialogue. For example, you might write:

> *Henry (despondently): No luck, Watson. We'll just have to –*
>
> *This represents the point in the narrative where they had just about given up hope of seeing Barrymore.*
>
> *The novel says: 'and we had almost for the second time given it up in despair, when in an instant…'*

Film version

As you learned in **Unit 8** (pages 50–55), a film-maker can use **montage**, **framing** and a variety of different **shots** to help tell the story clearly and excitingly.

1 Write notes on how:

- the montage in shots 141–147 helps show the sudden change from disappointment to excitement

- the montage in shots 148–151 gets across the idea that the men have passed through different parts of the house

- the framing in shot 148 shows how close behind Barrymore Sir Henry is

- the variety of different shots in frames 153–158 adds to the suspense (about who Barrymore is signalling to, and how he will react when he is caught)

2 Draw a rough storyboard of any six frames to show what the audience might see. Look back to pages 38–39 to remind yourself how to add notes. Add timings to show how long you think each shot should take. (Look at the notes and timings for *Frankenstein* and *Macbeth* on pages 50–51 and 56–57 to give you some ideas.)

5 Planning your own media work

Here is the section from *The Hound of the Baskervilles* which follows the extract on page 63. Write two adaptations of it: one for radio and one for film.

'What are you doing here, Barrymore?'

'Nothing, sir.' His agitation was so great that he could hardly speak, and the shadows sprang up and down from the shaking of his candle. 'It was the window, sir. I go round at night to see that they are fastened.'

'On the second floor?'

'Yes, sir, all the windows.'

'Look here, Barrymore,' said Sir Henry sternly, 'we have made up our minds to have the truth out of you, so it will save you the trouble to tell it sooner rather than later. Come now! No lies! What were you doing at that window?'

The fellow looked at us in a helpless way, and he wrung his hands together like one who is in the last extremity of doubt and misery.

'I was doing no harm, sir. I was holding a candle to the window.'

'And why were you holding a candle to the window?'

'Don't ask me, Sir Henry – don't ask me! I give you my word, sir, that it is not my secret, and that I cannot tell it. If it concerned no one but myself I would not try to keep it from you.'

A sudden idea occurred to me, and I took the candle from the window-sill where the butler had placed it.

'He must have been holding it up as a signal,' said I. 'Let us see if there is any answer.'

I held it up as he had done, and stared out into the darkness of the night. Vaguely I could discern the black bank of the trees and the lighter expanse of the moor, for the moon was behind the clouds. And then I gave a cry of exultation, for a tiny pin-point of

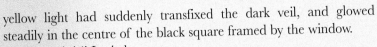

yellow light had suddenly transfixed the dark veil, and glowed steadily in the centre of the black square framed by the window.

'There it is!' I cried.

Arthur Conan Doyle

STARTING POINTS

- Remember that:

  a listening audience can only know what is happening through the dialogue and the sound effects;

  films, on the other hand, tell most of their story through images, rather than words.

- In preparing to write a radio script, you might find it helpful to read the extract through in a group, taking the parts of Barrymore, Watson and Sir Henry.

- To get some ideas about a film version, you could sketch out a sequence of storyboard frames.

CLUES FOR SUCCESS

- **For radio**, think about the ways in which a sound effect can help the listeners to know:

  what the characters are doing (through the sound of footsteps or a scuffle, for example)

  how much time has passed (a clock chiming, a cock crowing...)

  where the scene is taking place (street noises, an owl hooting...)

- **For film**, remember the variety of techniques film-makers use, to do with:

  the camera: including camera angles, cutting, montage, framing, varying shots, lighting, timing

  sound: sound effects, music

  location: props and costumes

  You might find it helpful to look back at the advice about planning a film at the end of Unit 8 (pages 54–55).

- **For both adaptations**, don't feel that you have to include every line of the novel's dialogue or every idea in the narrative – all adaptations have to cut some of the original book. At the same time you might find it helpful – especially in the radio adaptation – to add some of your own dialogue in order to make clear to the audience what is going on. But, if you do that, make it sound as much like Conan Doyle's dialogue as possible.

MEDIA FRAME

Here is one frame to start you off. It gives you advice on layout and shows you some of the techniques you can use in adapting the story for the medium of radio and film.

Adapting the *Hound of the Baskervilles* for radio

Script	Layout	Technique
Barrymore (*frightened*): Nothing sir. [*Brief silence*] It-it was the window, sir. I go round at night to see that they are fastened.	• no speech marks • stage directions in brackets and in italics	The frightened tone in the actor's voice will let the audience know how he is reacting. The silence and the added hesitation (*It-it*) suggest that he is trying to think up a convincing story.
Sir Henry (*disbelieving*): On the second floor?		
Barrymore Yes, sir, all the windows. [*FX: determined footsteps across the room*]		The sound effect helps us to imagine Sir Henry's movement towards Barrymore.

 REDRAFTING AND IMPROVING

Look back at your two adaptations. Check that you have:

• thought carefully about how to tell the story in the medium

• used a variety of radio techniques in each medium

• used a variety of radio and film techniques

6 ❯ **Looking back**

When they are adapting a novel for a different medium:

• **radio playwrights** depend upon dialogue and sound effects to tell the story

• **film-makers** use a variety of visual and sound techniques

Ways of selling

1 ▷ **Purpose**

In this unit you will:

- see how Clarks shoes are advertised in magazines and on television
- study the different methods used by the two advertisements
- design two advertisements for a new product: one to go in a magazine; the other to appear on television

➤➤ **Subject links:** *PSHE, media studies*

2 ▷ **Comparing print-media and television advertising**

How to get your new shoes noticed.

Wear correct trousers. Set up a display in your window. Walk on your hands.

Act your shoe size, not your age.

How to get your new shoes noticed

Here are two advertisements for a new range of Clarks shoes. The first appeared in several magazines; the second on television.

The magazine advertisement took up a whole page and looked like this.

The television advertisement lasted 29 seconds and was in four sections.

Section 1 *(0–8 seconds)*

- A sequence of shots of boys playing football in a park. In the background is the faint sound of their shouts.

- This cuts briefly to a shot of a smartly-dressed young man in casual clothes strolling along a path near where the boys are playing.

- Back to the boys, and one of them kicks the ball hard. It flies off in the direction of the path.

- Over the next few shots, it looks as though the man is going to helpfully trap the ball and kick it back. But he lifts his foot and lets it roll away underneath.

There is a clear shot of the man's shoes as he lifts his foot to let the ball pass underneath.

- The final frames of Section 1 show the boys looking disgusted and the man looking smug as he strolls on.

Section 2 *(9–19 seconds)*

- Two women are standing in front of the mirrors in a washroom, checking their hair and make-up. There is no sound except for their footsteps on the tiled floor.

- When one leaves, the other looks round and dodges into one of the cubicles opposite, leaving the door open.

She stands on the toilet bowl and poses in front of the mirror opposite, admiring her shoes.

Section 3 *(20–25 seconds)*

- A woman is sitting outside a pavement café reading a newspaper. There is a faint sound of traffic in the background.

There is a shot from her point of view, as she admires her shoes.

- She peeps over the top of her paper.

Section 4 *(26–29 seconds)*

- A shot from above of a pair of new Clarks shoes in their open box. A voice says 'New shoes...'

- Cut to a shot from the same angle, but with the lid on. The voice gives a sigh of pleasure: 'Aaaah!'

3 ▷ **Key features**

Both advertisements:

- try to get across the idea that there is something very special about Clarks shoes

- use clever, unusual images to get the messages across

- include a slogan or catchphrase

4 > Media skills

All advertisements are aimed at a particular audience. They are known as the **target group**. For example, television advertisements for computer games are aimed mainly at boys up to 15 years old; most shampoo advertisements are aimed at women in the 16–35 age group. When a new advertisement is being planned, the makers have to ask themselves at least two questions:

- which gender are we aiming at:
  male
  female
  or both?

- which age group are we aiming at:
  up to 15
  16–24
  25–35
  36–55
  over 55?

1 Write down examples of television or magazine advertisements for particular products which might be aimed at each of the following target groups:

- boys 13–15 years
- girls 13–15
- men 25–55
- women 16–24
- men and women over 55

2 The two Clarks advertisements are probably aimed at the same target groups. Look at the images and the humorous approach, and decide which target groups they are.

The **message** of an advertisement is the main point that the advertisers are trying to get across. Most advertisements deliver a very simple message, such as: *our supermarket is the cheapest* or *you can't tell the difference between our spread and real butter.*

3 Here are six advertising messages about Clarks shoes. In pairs decide which one you think is the message for the magazine advertisement and which for the television advertisement.

If you buy Clarks shoes, you will:
- *find them really comfortable*
- *want people to notice them*
- *get a lot of use out of them*
- *want to keep looking at them yourself*
- *be envied by all your friends*
- *be stared at in the street*

An **image** is a picture used by an advertiser to achieve a particular effect. Advertisers choose images very carefully in order to get particular messages across.

4 In pairs, look at the main image in the magazine advertisement (a pair of shoes in their box). Which camera shot has been used (long-shot, close-up…)?

5 Make notes on the framing and the camera angle (such as: from the side or from straight above). Decide what effect is achieved by choosing that particular shot, framing and camera angle.

6 Ask yourselves the same questions about the three smaller images at the bottom. In each case, what is the effect of choosing that particular shot, framing and angle?

A **caption** is a short piece of writing which explains, or comments on, a particular image.

The three smaller images at the foot of the magazine advertisement each have a caption. The image and caption together each give a humorous example of *How to get your new shoes noticed*.

7 Make up another caption which might have been used in this advertisement. Draw a sketch of the image to go with it. Notice that the caption needs to begin with an imperative verb (see page 34), such as *wear*, *set up* or *walk*. Here is an example, to give you an idea:

Display them in an art gallery

Print-media texts (anything that appears on a page) and moving-image texts (such as films or television advertisements) are very different. One major difference is that moving-image texts have **duration**. That means that the film-maker has to think about how much time to give to each shot.

The television advertisement for Clarks shoes is almost half a minute long and each of the three 'scenes' takes several seconds.

8 These questions will help you to think about duration in moving-image texts. Discuss them in pairs and come up with approximate answers.

- What is the longest film you have watched?
- How long do you think the average television advertisement is:
  – when school-age viewers are expected to be watching?
  – later in the evening?
- How many seconds did Cantona's flying kick last in the sequence on pages 44–45?
- How long was the opening of the film of *Macbeth* (pages 56–57)? How many seconds did it take for the witches to speak Shakespeare's lines?
- How many seconds were left after the captain spoke the final words in *Frankenstein* (page 51)?

5 ▷ Planning your own writing

Write an article which compares the magazine advertisement for Clarks shoes with the television advertisement.

▶ STARTING POINTS

- First make notes on all the things that the two advertisements have in common. For example, to begin with, they are probably aimed at the same target groups.

- Then note down all the differences. It will help to look back at the section on duration (on page 77).

▶ CLUES FOR SUCCESS

Use what you have learned from the activities on:

- target groups
- an advertisement's message
- images
- captions and slogans
- montage, framing and camera angles
- duration of shots

▶ REDRAFTING AND IMPROVING

Check that you have:

- covered all the different features dealt with in the **Media skills** section

- supported your points by referring closely to particular details of each advertisement

▶▶ WRITING FRAME

	Structure	Look back at activities
Comparing the two advertisements	Introduction	1, 2
	Paragraph 2	3
	Paragraph 3	4, 5, 6
		7
	Paragraph 4	8
	Paragraph 5	
	Conclusion	

- pointed out similarities and differences between the two advertisements

- shown how each advertisement is designed to get the most out of its particular medium

Content	Suggested phrases
• the product	*The two advertisements are both for the same product...*
• the target groups	*In both cases the target groups are probably...*
• the main messages of the two advertisements	*Each advertisement has its own message...*
• the difference between the messages	*The difference is that...*
• how the images help to get those messages across	*The main image of the magazine advertisement is...* *On the other hand...*
• how the captions and slogans are used in the magazine advertisement	*The captions are important because...* *Both advertisements conclude with a slogan*
• the use of montage, framing, camera angles and duration of shots in the TV ad	*The makers of the television advertisement employ a number of techniques to convey the message that...*
• any other points	*One final point is that...*
• how each of the advertisements is designed to get the most out of its particular medium	*The makers of these two advertisements have skilfully exploited the strengths of each medium...*

6 ▷ Looking back

- Products can be advertised in print media – such as newspapers, magazines and leaflets – and moving-image media – such as film and television.

- The advertisers will always have a **target group** in mind.

- Print-media texts and moving-image texts are very different. One of the major differences is that moving-image texts have **duration**.

Glossary

Angles Camera shots from different directions and heights.

Caption A short piece of writing which explains, or comments on, an image.

Casting The choice of actors to play particular parts.

Colloquial language Vocabulary and expressions which are closer to everyday, informal speech.

Copy The written text in an advertisement. The main block of copy is known as the body copy.

Cutting The skill of changing from one film shot to another.

Duration The dimension of time in moving-image texts.

Editing The skill of selecting, and joining, camera shots.

Emotive words Words which have a particular effect on our feelings.

Frame A single image on a strip of film.

Framing The skill of placing people or objects in different positions within the edges of the film frame to get particular effects.

Genres The different kinds of books and films with their own special features.

Graphics The art of putting images and lettering together for a special effect.

Image A picture used by an advertiser to achieve a particular effect.

Interpretation Somebody's idea of what a book, play or film means.

Intro The opening paragraph or sentence of a newspaper article.

Location The place where a scene is filmed.

Logo A special symbol which represents a large organisation such as a business, a charity or a college.

Media Sources of information, advertising and entertainment, such as the press, television, cinema or the Internet. Print media include newspapers, magazines and posters. Moving-image media include films, television and video.

Montage The skill of joining moving-image shots together to achieve a particular effect.

Parody A comedy film or book which mocks the typical features of a particular genre.

Props Short for *properties* – all the hand-held objects used in a play.

Quotes Someone's exact words.

Register The style of language we choose, to suit a particular situation or a certain kind of subject matter.

Rhyme The effect achieved by using words with the same, or similar, sounds.

Sequence A series of frames which tells part of a story, such as a whole scene.

Shot A single, uninterrupted run of the camera.

Slogan A short, catchy phrase designed to stick in the memory.

Stage directions Information given to people performing the play to help them to understand how it can be acted.

Target group The particular audience at which an advertisement is aimed.

Typography The way words are typed, drawn or printed.